Outside the Whale

Outside the Whale:

George Orwell's Art and Politics

DAVID L. KUBAL

UNIVERSITY OF NOTRE DAME PRESS
NOTRE DAME   LONDON

Library of Congress Catalog Card Number: 72-3509
Manufactured in the United States of America by
NAPCO Graphic Arts, Inc., New Berlin, Wisconsin

To
ALL MY TEACHERS,
ESPECIALLY THE FIRST ONES:

Lawrence and Ruth Hayes Kubal

For the fact is that being inside a whale is a very comfortable, cosy, homelike thought. The historical Jonah, if he can be so called, was glad enough to escape, but in imagination, day-dream, countless people have envied him. It is, of course, quite obvious why. The whale's belly is simply a womb big enough for an adult. There you are, in the dark, cushioned space that exactly fits you, with yards of blubber between yourself and reality, able to keep up an attitude of the completest indifference, no matter what happens.

GEORGE ORWELL
"Inside the Whale"

Contents

Acknowledgments

Parts of chapter two and chapter three appeared originally in somewhat different versions in *The Midwest Quarterly*, the *Arizona Quarterly*, and *The University Review*. I thank the editors of the journals for their kind permission to reprint these sections.

Of the many who have helped me in the making of this book I would like particularly to mention Miss Ann Rice of the University of Notre Dame Press, who with her notes and kind queries made the last few months less painful; and Professors Peter A. Brier and John C. Bushman of California State University, Los Angeles, who cheerfully read proofs.

With special gratitude I thank Professor Joseph M. Duffy, Jr., of the University of Notre Dame, who respected my opinions from the beginning and encouraged me in difficult times; and Professor Otto W. Fick of California State University, Los Angeles, who gave me invaluable advice on revision.

To Professor James L. McDonald of the University of Detroit, who believes that games are the way to sanity, I owe my endurance. To Catherine, Elizabeth, and John, who think closed doors are to be opened, I owe my balance. To Cynthia, who listened patiently and understood, simply—I owe much.

Introduction

A key to the character of the modern literary imagination is found in chapter 4 of James Joyce's *A Portrait of the Artist as a Young Man*. Before Stephen Dedalus rejects his priestly vocation for that of the artist, the narrator says about his hero, "In vague sacrificial or sacramental acts alone his will seemed drawn to go forth to encounter reality: and it was partly the absence of an appointed rite which had always constrained him to inaction whether he had allowed silence to cover his anger or pride or had suffered only an embrace he longed to give."[1] Deciding that the priesthood does not offer the freedom he seeks, Dedalus embraces the life of art which allows him, at last, "to go forth to encounter reality," if not immediately, eventually in *Ulysses*.

The modern artist, like Dedalus, seeks "an appointed rite," a form to give shape to his experience, to free him from old, invalid forms and to allow him to act, to create. George Orwell, a member of the modern movement's second generation, found himself in a predicament similar to that of Dedalus and Joyce. Alienated from family, class, religion, and homeland, he too sought a form which would satisfy him both as a man and an artist. Yet the state of exile which he experienced in Burma, Paris, and London, was no longer, he felt, a viable one. Nor, given the economic and political conditions of his time, could he affirm an aesthetic order as a solution of his own sense of fragmentation. On the contrary, he realized that only in the creation of some type of political form or myth could he "go forth to encounter reality."

I think it must be stressed that Dedalus required a myth not only to deal with experience as an artist but also—as the narrator makes clear—in order to overcome his loneliness and to engage with humanity, which he finally does by sharing a cup of cocoa with Leopold Bloom. This is the point W. B. Yeats makes in "Ego Dominus Tuus," in which he justifies the creation of his "Vision" by pointing out that if the poet bases his art solely on the self, his creative resources will dry up and he will be left an isolated man. The modern artist's quest is an integral one; it is a seeking after an "otherness" which provides a source for his art apart from the self and at the same time furnishes an identity in and with the community at large.

In his search Orwell, like many middle-class intellectuals of his generation, rejected all the old political myths as untenable in a time of crisis. But he did not, in his desperation, align himself with any of the new myths. Both his inquiry and eventual solution were of a highly eclectic nature, and consequently his ideas often appear paradoxical and even contradictory. As an artist his situation was even more complicated. In view of the political danger of his age, he felt that the writer no longer had the choice of ignoring social reality. Rather, he had the moral responsibility to warn and inform—that is, he had the duty to propagandize. But he never advocated that the artist subordinate his aesthetic responsibility to his political one; he must instead find a way to bring the two purposes into an intelligent whole.

Thus Orwell's artistic search was parallel and analogous to his political-personal quest: Both had as their ends a form which would structure contemporary experience. And indeed, as I will argue, only when Orwell constructs his own version of a political myth is he able to move beyond himself and mature as an artist. Nor is it a coincidence that these phenomena should occur concurrently: Both Joyce and Yeats achieved the stature of major artists only after they were able to create a myth which established the relationship between the self, society, and the historical process.

Through this comparison I am not suggesting that Orwell's achievement as an artist equals that of Joyce or Yeats. Yet in many ways he remains for us a more relevant figure than either of them. He has been called "the conscience of his generation" as well as a saint. Such reactions—often verging on a veneration which Orwell would not have understood—stem from a recognition of his willingness to face himself and the realities of his time with stubborn honesty. His honesty had a quality that led Richard Rees, perhaps his closest confident, to describe him as a "fugitive from the camp of victory." For Orwell, truth was finally more precious than the sanctity or security of any system of belief. Lies, no matter how useful to the cause, could never achieve anything but a form of totalitarianism. His fellow Socialists, therefore, were no safer from his scrutiny than the Tories or Fascists.

His willingness to remain critically outside and to maintain his objectivity, even if it hindered the "progress" of socialism, angered many. The diatribe of the Columbia graduate student in Saul Bellow's novel, *Mr. Sammler's Planet,* is similar to the invective frequently used to describe Orwell by the radical Socialists during the late thirties and forties. The student calls out:

> "Old Man! You quoted Orwell before."
> "Yes?"
> "You quoted him to say that British radicals were all protected by the Royal Navy? Did Orwell say that British Radicals were protected by the Royal Navy?"
> "Yes, I believe he did say that."
> "That's a lot of shit."
> Sampler could not speak.
> "Orwell was a fink. He was a sick counterrevolutionary. It's good he died when he did."[2]

If Orwell's inconsistencies and eclecticism enrage those who are willing to barter objectivity for the security of a faith, his devotion to fact rather than ideological consistency endears him to those who believe that all orthodoxies or rigid myths ultimately deprive the self of its freedom. We might view him, then, as the devil's advocate, an attacker of all the desperate, obsessive beliefs of what W. H. Auden called that "low dishonest decade." But Orwell, in many senses the first contemporary writer and thinker, also realized that the individual must create a framework of meaning if he is to remain human, while at the same time he must learn to exist beyond the comforting shadow of the absolutes. As I have pointed out, he saw the necessity of such a meaning as a support for both his art and life. His struggle was painful and at last indecisive; it was not an insignificant one, however, if we judge the value of his search rather than its success.

PART ONE
POLITICS

The Political Odyssey

I

The complexion and direction of George Orwell's politics are intelligible only if we understand his sense of the moral vacuum in modern culture, that Western civilization as it existed was no longer viable. Although not an admirer of W. B. Yeats, he did appreciate "The Second Coming." Reviewing a critical study of Yeats during the Second World War and commenting on that poem, he wrote, "He is too big a man to share the illusions of Liberalism, and as early as 1920 he foretells in a justly famous passage . . . the kind of world we have actually moved into."[1] The determinism implicit in Yeats's view of history never attracted Orwell, but he did believe that we were living at the end of an era and that a decision had to be made. The

drift toward totalitarianism could only be stemmed
if the structure of society were radically changed.

At the beginning of the war in attempting to explain
why many British intellectuals had turned to the Communist party in the 1930s, Orwell observes that the
values of liberal-Christian culture could no longer
attract belief. But the dismissal of certain beliefs, as
he notes, does not eliminate the need for a faith. A
number of his peers, such as Stephen Spender and
C. Day Lewis, had turned to Soviet Marxism for a
country as well as a religion.[2] But for Orwell it could
not furnish a substitute; he was temperamentally incapable of accepting its rigid discipline and suppression
of the individual mind. Further, he realized before
most others that Russian communism had led to a
society not greatly different from Hitler's Third Reich.

His political search, then, was an attempt to find
a basis for civilization, a new myth, for he believed
that liberalism was untenable and communistic socialism, a fraud. The difficulty of his task is clear. Caught
between two worlds, the traditional in decay on one
side and the threat of totalitarianism on the other, he
had no formulated alternative to fall back upon. In
view of his predicament, the fact that he did not
despair and did ultimately manage to create out of
the ruins, so to speak, a moral basis for his socialism is a tribute to his integrity and intellectual
resourcefulness.

But before Orwell came to any decision about what
he felt could be a foundation for an equitable society,
before he even considered socialism as a solution, he
underwent his own disillusionment. He himself points

out that it was not until 1936 that he reached a decision about socialism.[3] And it was only after his experiences in the Spanish Civil War that his acceptance became final. In August 1937 he wrote to Cyril Connolly from Barcelona, "I have seen wonderful things & at last really believe in Socialism, which I never did before."[4] Between 1922, when he left Eton for Burma, and the middle thirties, he experienced the breakup of liberal culture at first hand in England, Burma, and on the Continent. After he returned from Burma in 1927, he sought experiences among the poor and down and out, whose existence demonstrated to him that Western civilization had, indeed, exhausted itself. But he was not simply seeking experience for its own sake but in order to discover, if possible, a bedrock for society.

Concluding from his life in England and Burma that the upper and middle classes were morally effete, he thought that among the working classes and the disinherited there might still remain a remnant of value. It seems that Orwell had an attraction, like his contemporary Graham Greene, for "the seedy," because as the latter says, "It is nearer the beginning; like Monrovia it has begun to build wrong, but at least it has only begun; it hasn't gone so far as the smart, the new, the chic, and the cerebral."[5] But it is not only the underdeveloped that has this quality for Greene; it is, as he notes, "even the seediness of civilisation, of the skysigns in Leicester Square, the 'tarts' in Bond Street, the smell of cooking greens off Tottenham Court Road, the motor salesmen in Great Portland Street. It seems to satisfy, temporarily, the sense of nostalgia for something lost; it seems to represent a stage further back" (pp. 7–8). In many ways Orwell's journey to the slums of Paris and London parallels Greene's trip to Africa. Essentially, both adventures originated in "a distrust of any future based on what we are" (p. 8).

Even though Orwell felt that liberal culture and its particular line of development could not provide the structure for a just community, he recognized certain values in that tradition which could not be dismissed. Indeed, he sought to preserve the liberal habit of mind with its belief in the objectivity of truth and in individual integrity. He realized the serious error made by the British Communists of the thirties in their ready acceptance of the shifting party line, their willingness to ignore or twist facts in the interest of unity. From the time he returned from Spain, Orwell continually pointed out that history was not something to be created but rather discovered. No matter how expedient, "organized lying," as he calls it in "The Prevention of Literature," is the foundation of totalitarianism.[6] If the concepts of objective truth and the right to dissent are eliminated from society, justice and equality will never be achieved: Cultural uniformity does not guarantee community, nor does the elimination of classes and economic imbalance without respect for the individual's rights assure freedom.

Orwell realized, moreover, a need for an orientation of individual freedom, something which traditional liberalism did not provide; he also knew that the purpose of society could not be defined in merely material or individual terms. On the other hand, he saw

that any orthodoxy which offered a moral direction
and a goal above the immediate and personal but at
the expense of truth and the integrity of the person
was equally enslaving. Conformity was not the answer
to cultural anarchy; both resulted in tyranny. While
the need for something to believe in may be a necessity, Orwell always insisted that personal freedom and
validity had a higher priority. To this extent, then, he
found meaning in liberalism, although its values were
not sufficient to form a political creed or myth, a fact
which was obvious enough in the failure of capitalistic
democracy. The necessity of a coherent and viable
morality still remained; a body of beliefs had to be
discovered or created to give direction and purpose to
the individual and society. In 1944 he wrote:

> I do not want the belief in life after death to return,
> and in any case it is not likely to return. What I do
> point out is that its disappearance has left a big hole,
> and that we ought to take notice of that fact. Reared
> for thousands of years on the notion that the individual
> survives, man has got to make a considerable psycho-
> logical effort to get used to the notion that the individ-
> ual perishes. He is not likely to salvage civilisation unless
> he can evolve a system of good and evil which is inde-
> pendent of heaven and hell.[7]

II

From the essay "Such, Such Were the Joys," published posthumously, we learn of Orwell's early disillusionment with his civilization's ethic, his first experience of tyranny as well as his sense of the incongruity

between what he perceived as the existing values and what he felt to be true. Certainly this feeling was clarified and perhaps even created to an extent by hindsight, since the essay was written nearly thirty years after the events.[8] Nevertheless, he writes of his school days at St. Cyprian's:

> I did not question the prevailing standards, because so far as I could see there were no others. How could the rich, the strong, the elegant, the fashionable, the powerful, be in the wrong? It was their world, and the rules they made for it must be the right ones. And yet from a very early age I was aware of the impossibility of any *subjective* conformity. Always at the centre of my heart the inner self seemed to be awake, pointing out the difference between the moral obligation and the psychological *fact*.[9]

Besides his failure to find an identity in his society, we see from this passage his initial feeling of vacuum—that there was nothing outside of himself, as far as he could see, which offered an alternative set of values. Even about a comparatively trivial matter such as physical appearance he felt bound to accept his peers' opinion. He says, "until after I had left school for good I continued to believe that I was preternaturally ugly. It was what my schoolfellows had told me, and I had no other authority to refer to" (p. 361).

But already at this point he discovered something which enabled him to withstand a tyrannical society. Indeed, he found within himself a capability which he would later translate into a political value. What emerged in his own character in the face of suppression and eventually what he saw in the working classes was the ability to endure; as he says, "I had nothing to help me except my dumb selfishness, my inability—not, indeed to despise myself, but to *dislike* myself—my instinct to survive" (p. 363). It is this capacity for surviving, which he first came upon in himself as a child, that he always maintained as the greatest weapon against totalitarianism and as a foundation for his socialism. In the essay "The Art of Donald McGill," he insists that "When it comes to the pinch, human beings are heroic. Women face childbed and the scrubbing brush, revolutionaries keep their mouths shut in the torture chamber, battleships go down with guns still firing when their decks are awash."[10]

This courageous spirit is precisely the moral quality he found in the characters which he encountered among society's outcasts and related in *Down and Out in Paris and London*. Unlike Boris, Paddy, and Bozo of that book, however, John Flory of *Burmese Days*, a middle-class, public-school Englishman, does not possess the inner resources to survive alienation and so commits suicide. Although he realizes imperialism is hypocritical, that it is, in reality, a politics of exploitation and that his colleagues' values are shallow and narrow, he himself has nothing to offer in their place except a kind of belated and unrealistic traditionalism. He wants to recreate the Burmese national character and return the country to its primitive culture, a reversion, ironically, that the native politicians, represented by the corrupt U Po Kyin, do not want. Under the pressures of the system Flory's moral character has deteriorated as well, and therefore he believes his only hope for survival is Elizabeth Lackersteen's love. He

is painfully wrong about her and never finally sees
that all she desires is to find a "respectable" husband
and to become a "burra memsahib." When Elizabeth
eventually rejects him, what he thinks is his last possibility disappears and he despairs.

Flory's predicament is similar to the narrator's in
"Shooting an Elephant," where Orwell dramatizes
even more pointedly the irony of the middle-class rise
to economic and political authority. The real nature
of imperialism, as the narrator of that essay learns,
is that the wielder of tyrannical power is himself en-
slaved. Knowing that he should not kill the elephant,
realizing that no purpose would be accomplished by
the slaughter, he yet shoots the animal because the
Burmese crowd expects it and he must save face as a
policeman. At the end he says, "I often wondered
whether any of the others grasped that I had done it
solely to avoid looking a fool."[11]

After a time, even though Flory sees through the
British justification of imperialism, he has become an
irrevocable part of the system. Consequently, any interior strength that he might have possessed has been
depleted. At last, Flory is a victim of his own class:
Brought up to believe in its righteousness and honesty,
he becomes aware of its hypocrisy when it is too late,
for he has been morally gelded; his individuality has
been absorbed by the organization. Flory's conscience,
in other words, has been totally objectivized and as
these external values lose their validity for him, he disintegrates. Not even the opportunity of salvation in
another person, much less a choice of another system,
remains. Unlike the lower classes, which have not been
taken into modern society and therefore have been

able to maintain a sense of community, the middle and upper classes provide no moral support for their members. The only choice offered is between conformity and social isolation, both fatal for Flory.

Burmese Days and its central character are based on Orwell's own experiences in the East. But there is an important difference in the ages of Flory and his creator. The former was in his middle thirties, while the latter was only twenty-four when he left Burma. Flory, therefore, might be seen as what Orwell feared he would have become if he had not left the service. Writing of his decision to give up his position as a policeman and go "down and out," he says,

> I felt that I had got to escape not merely from imperialism but from every form of man's dominion over man. I wanted to submerge myself, to get right down among the oppressed, to be one of them and on their side against their tyrants. And, chiefly because I had had to think everything out in solitude, I had carried my hatred of oppression to extraordinary lengths. At that time failure seemed to me to be the only virtue. Every suspicion of self-advancement, even to "succeed" in life to the extent of making a few hundreds a year, seemed to me spiritually ugly, a species of bullying.
>
> It was in this way that my thoughts turned towards the English working class.[12]

And so his choice assumes a number of meanings. First of all, his descent has mythic significance: It is a journey into the underworld, both of the self and of civilization, where he hopes to "think everything out in solitude" in order to reconstruct a new self. He planned, as he says, "how one could sell everything, give everything away, change one's name and start out with no money and nothing but the clothes one stood up in" (p. 151). This attempt to de-class himself also resembles a rite of purification. His duties as a policeman left him with acute guilt feelings, which he sought to purge by identifying himself with the oppressed: "I could go among these people, see what their lives were like and feel myself temporarily part of their world. Once I had been among them and accepted by them, I should have touched bottom, and —this is what I felt: I was aware even then that it was irrational—part of my guilt would drop from me" (p. 151).

Besides an attempt to make contact with the working class, an element in society which had not been corrupted by the modern ethic, his journey was also a search for inner energy which would enable him, unlike Flory, to survive. The fact that he published *Burmese Days* in 1934, only after he had undergone his experience in the "underworld," seems to indicate he had successfully achieved a new identity, allowing him the necessary objectivity. The central importance of *Down and Out* for understanding Orwell's politics is obvious. Although in the early thirties, he had, as he later admitted, no "interest in Socialism," he did become "aware" for the first time of the working class, whose values would become the basis for political hope. More immediately, he discovered the existence of an alternative to the middle-class world and Flory's final "solution."

* * *

In Orwell's second novel, *A Clergyman's Daughter*, published in 1935, the protagonist also finds the strength for endurance after contact with the working class. Dorothy Hare, the only daughter of a widowed, self-indulgent Anglican curate, has constructed her life and faith on weak, wooden habits. No more than an automaton, she lives by religious catchphrases which she has never questioned. A sudden loss of memory, however, strips Dorothy of all fictitious supports, her faith and routine parish duties, which have given her life some sort of order. Thrown into the nether world of London among migrant workers, bums, and prostitutes, she must learn how to cope with existence and how simply to stay alive. The only fact she knows with any certainty is that she does not believe in anything. When she regains her memory, Dorothy finds she cannot go back to her father because of a scandal about her and an older man, Mr. Warburton. Eventually she is rescued from a police court by a rich uncle and sent to teach in a tenth-rate private girl's school. After nearly a year of teaching, where she learns, as Orwell himself did, that the sole motive behind this type of lower-middle-class school is profit, she returns to her father.

But Dorothy cannot reembrace the old faith. About the only thing which has remained intact after her exile is, inexplicably, her virginity. Bereft of former belief, she is confronted with absolute emptiness. On the other hand, she has discovered during her "descent" that she is able to exist on her own. She uncovers in herself the disinherited's ability to live without meaning, to survive despite inhuman conditions. At the end she even refuses any substitute for her lost faith: "no pagan acceptance of life as sufficient to itself, no pantheistic cheer-up stuff, no pseudo-religion of 'progress' with visions of glittering Utopias and ant-heaps of steel and concrete. It is all or nothing. Either life on earth is a preparation for something greater and more lasting, or it is meaningless, dark and dreadful."[13] But she does resume her responsibilities as a "clergyman's daughter," because in that, she begins to see, remains her "salvation."

Orwell appears to be advocating here a species of Conrad's "work-ethic," which we can understand as a devotion to the immediate and the particular in the interests of survival. For as the narrator says about Dorothy: "She did not reflect, consciously, that the solution to her difficulty lay in accepting the fact that there was no solution; that if one gets on with the job that lies to hand, the ultimate purpose of the job fades into insignificance; that faith and no faith are very much the same provided that one is doing what is customary, useful and acceptable" (pp. 318–319). In the end Dorothy turns to the task of making costumes for the church play. "The problem of faith and no faith had vanished utterly from her mind. It was beginning to get dark, but, too busy to stop and light the lamp, she worked on, pasting strip after strip of paper into place, with absorbed, with pious concentration, in the penetrating smell of the gluepot" (p. 320).

Dorothy is able to achieve what Flory could not. And in view of the circumstances, her rejection of any form of escapism or self-deception and the fact that she doesn't despair is an accomplishment. Both she and Flory are of the "solid" middle class, but Dorothy has the additional experience of the subterranean world where she becomes aware of an alternative to the values of her class or total negation. Like Orwell at school, she insists on the self and declines the possibility of defeat. This virtue—call it stubbornness—is paltry salvage from the humanistic tradition; it is only a fragment, but it is also a possible beginning.

III

After Orwell's experiments among the working class there never appeared any doubt in his mind about man's talent for *survival*. But there was one concerning humanity's ability to *prevail*, which is, of course, the ultimate political question. Dorothy Hare's situation is only bearable, and her attitude, like the dispossessed's, has only minimal political worth. He was neither naïve nor sentimental about the workingman, who, as he realized, could resist tyranny but did not have sufficient creativity nor intelligence to remake society. Unfortunately, he felt, the British intellectuals had sold out either to their own class or to the Communist party, or like Henry Miller, they had gone "inside the whale," withdrawing from politics and society. In *The Road to Wigan Pier*, therefore, he sought to persuade the Socialists to rid themselves of obvious eccentrics in order to attract both the intellectuals and the middle class. Even before he wrote that book, however, he began to understand the necessity of certain middle-class virtues. And this marks a change, if a qualified one, in his thinking.

Richard Rees, a coeditor of *Adelphi*, for which Orwell reviewed early in his career, relates an incident that took place during the middle thirties. Orwell was introduced to a militant Communist who proceeded to berate the bourgeois. Irritated by his jargon, Orwell said, " 'Look here, I'm a bourgeois and my family are bourgeois. If you talk about them like that I'll punch your head.' "[14] This new attitude toward his own class appears quite vividly in his third novel, *Keep the Aspidistra Flying*, published in 1936. As Christopher Hollis says, it is in this book that one finds "Orwell's definitive rejection of the ambition to de-class himself."[15] The publication of *Keep the Aspidistra Flying* also coincided with his marriage to Eileen O'Shaughnessy in June 1936; afterwards they settled down to run a village shop at Wallington in Hertfordshire. They planned to open the general store only in the afternoons so that he could write in the mornings. It was definitely, as Rees notes, the beginning of a more "cheerful period" in his life.[16]

Orwell's acceptance of the middle class, however, had certain qualifications. As much as he desired a classless community, he was sensitive to the various divisions in society. In *The Road to Wigan Pier* he defines his own origins as the "clerks" of the empire, the lower part of the upper middle class, "which had its heyday in the 'eighties and 'nineties . . ." and was now a "sort of mound of wreckage left behind when the tide of Victorian prosperity receded" (p. 123). And so it was not the upper or higher segments of the middle class, themselves part of the decayed power structure, which he thought had anything to contribute to his idea of socialism. It was not the administrators or managers but the working, lower middle class which still held to the ideas of family and traditional morality. This class, he felt, had maintained the old English virtues and had not allowed itself to be totally absorbed into the twentieth century. If he ended the attempt to become a workingman, he did not do so to return to his original class. T. R. Fyvel, a friend of Orwell, asserts that he changed his name from Eric Blair to define a "new social status for himself."[17] He sought, in short, a new identity—at least for a time— among shopkeepers.

Gordon Comstock, the central figure of *Keep the Aspidistra Flying*, tries to defy society, as Orwell did, by embracing failure. Orwell's "submergence," however, was not self-destructive; it was undertaken for positive reasons, such as the desire to expiate guilt, to make contact with the workingman, and to discover himself. Comstock, the last member of an enervated middle-class family, feels that there is nothing in contemporary society to equal his talents, and so he goes under. But the mystique of failure is nothing more than a reveling in self-pity, an adolescent gesture of defeatism designed to avoid responsibility. It is not a sign of strength but rather of moral exhaustion; akin to Flory's final act, it is a surrender, an admission that one can no longer control his own life. The acceptance of failure constitutes the last gasp of the shallow liberal imagination confronted by hard fact.

The reconstruction of Gordon's will is carried out through the agency of Rosemary Waterloo, a name of obvious significance. Freely giving herself without fear of the consequences when he is on the verge of final disintegration, Rosemary becomes pregnant. She then presents him with the choices of abortion, having the child out of wedlock, or marriage and a return to his former advertising job. He accepts the last course, because, as he sees, it has something to do with life.

By the middle 1930s the moral basis of Orwell's socialism began to take shape. Eclectic in nature, it borrowed the bare instinct of survival from the working classes and the "respectable" virtues from the bourgeois. The minority elements in society were insufficient by themselves, because by living in poverty, they had lost control of their lives. But the lower middle class had the means to retain a certain independence. It had, in other terms, the constitutional ability to prevail. As Lionel Trilling asserts, Orwell's

> clear, uncanting mind saw that, although the morality of history might come to harsh conclusions about the middle class and although the practicality of history might say that its day was over, there yet remained the considerable residue of its genuine virtues. The love of personal privacy, of order, of manners, the ideal of fairness and responsibility—these are very simple virtues indeed and they scarcely constitute perfection of either the personal or the social life. Yet they still might serve to judge the present and to control the future.[18]

Missing, nevertheless, from the combination of the working- and middle-class virtues is creative intelligence, the ability to conceptualize and give shape to history. According to Orwell, however, the intellectual separated from his own culture, from the moral energy of society, had no direction. His principal political problem, therefore, was to bring together knowledge and morality; or putting it in practical terms: to eliminate class barriers. On the one hand, the working and middle classes were suspicious of the intellectual; while, on the other, the educated had an aversion for the lower classes. Totalitarianism could neither be averted nor democratic socialism established unless these resources could be unified. Recognizing this and his responsibility as an intellectual, Orwell could not remain a shopkeeper. William Morris's socialism was not realistic in the twentieth century, if indeed it ever had been. Therefore early in 1936 Orwell investigated conditions in the north of England for the Left Book Club and in December of that year left Hertfordshire for Spain to fight fascism.

*   *   *

His experiences in industrial England and in Spain, retold in *The Road to Wigan Pier* and *Homage to Catalonia* and published in 1937 and 1938, respectively, confirmed his own thinking about socialism. Before he went to the north he had lived among capitalism's outcasts, those who merely existed on the fringe. But in Yorkshire and Lancashire he came to know the victimized who were actually inside the system, the coal miners and mill hands living on one or two pounds a week. Capitalism appeared to him, as well as to others in the thirties, to be in its last stage rather than in a period preceding readjustment and change.

Primarily, however, he sensed decay both in the public and personal life of the workers. The moral breakup he had dramatized in his previous writings assumed a new dimension in light of his findings in the huge industrial centers. It was not only the class system which pepetuated imperialism, poverty, and the money code, but also economic *laissez-faire*. It is true he had understood the *plongeurs* in Paris hotels and the tramps in London as products of a diseased economy. But in taking the road to Wigan, he was, in a manner of speaking, following capitalism to its sources. For the first time he himself encountered industrialism, the basis of modern civilization.

Like most of Orwell's works, *Wigan Pier*, then, entails an expedition into the interior. Although not as much a personal journey as the one described in *Down and Out*, this "road" does end in his belief in socialism as the only cure for, and replacement of, capitalism. But it is evident, from Victor Gollancz's explanatory foreword to the Left Book Club edition of *Wigan Pier*,[19] that he did not simply accept the socialist line. It was with some very definite reservations that he aligned himself with its ideas. Gollancz found his reports on conditions in the first half of the book moving and accurate. In the second half, to which the publisher objected, Orwell advocated socialism but also criticized several aspects of the movement. For the most part, he disagreed with its reliance on the machine in its plans for the future. Not a Luddite, he understood there was no question of "scrapping the machine" or industrialism, but he did think "that Socialism, as usually presented, is bound up with the idea of mechanical progress, not merely as a necessary development, but as an end in itself, almost as a kind of religion" (p. 188).

This conviction, together with socialism's faith in

materialism, its dependency on abstract thought, and his observation that a large number of Socialists were faddists and cranks, alienated him from the party. If socialism were to create a moral framework for the future and attract the working and middle classes, as was necessary for success, certain changes would have to be made. In its present state, again according to Orwell, socialism was not leading man toward freedom but rather toward fascism. As he says:

> We have got to admit that if Fascism is everywhere advancing, that is largely the fault of Socialists themselves. Partly it is due to the mistaken Communist tactic of sabotaging democracy, i.e., sawing off the branch you are sitting on; but still more to the fact that Socialists have, so to speak, presented their case wrong side foremost. They have never made it sufficiently clear that the essential aims of Socialism are justice and liberty. With their eyes glued to economic facts, they have proceeded on the assumption that man has no soul, and explicitly or implicitly they have set up the goal of a materialistic Utopia. As a result Fascism has been able to play upon every instinct that revolts against hedonism and a cheap conception of "progress." (p. 212)

When one attempts to define Orwell's socialism, he must always remember it is a highly individualized idea, constructed from diverse sources, rather than a single orthodoxy. Yet one of the deficiencies of *Wigan Pier* is that he had nothing more definite to offer in the place of the socialism he rejected than an idea based on "justice and liberty." He could articulate what socialism was *not*. At this time, however, he had not formulated anything very positive. He did not, of course, experience a total commitment to socialism until he went to Spain. Intellectually, he realized it was the only possible alternative to tyranny, whatever its brand. As he says at the end of *Wigan Pier:* "There is no chance of righting the conditions I described in the earlier chapters of this book, or of saving England from Fascism, unless we can bring an effective Socialist party into existence" (p. 228–229). What remained for him was to bring together the remnants of faith which he had managed to salvage into some kind of systematic coherence, or at least as close to a system as his skepticism would allow. A catalyst, obviously, was needed. Fortunately, at this critical juncture in his life the opportunity to go to Spain appeared.

* * *

Before the Spanish Civil War, Orwell never managed to involve himself totally in the life of the common man, to feel that a community without class barriers was a possibility. Even during his excursions among the lower classes there always remained in him a partial feeling of exclusion and masquerade. This is vividly brought out in another amusing but significant anecdote. Richard Rees tells how Orwell arrived at his flat one day and changed from his "respectable" suit into rags. He says Orwell "wanted . . . to know about prison from the inside and he hoped that if he were picked up drunk and disorderly in the East End he might manage to achieve this. Next day he reappeared very crestfallen. He had duly got drunk and been taken to a police station. But once there he had received a fatherly talk, spent the night in a cell and been let out the next morning with a cup of tea and some good advice."[20] His manner and accent accounted, I suppose, for his quick release. But, in Spain, when he joined a P.O.U.M. unit, a Trotskyite brigade the majority of whom were Spanish workers rather than Englishmen, all distinction was erased.

Despite the real sense of community based on socialistic principles which he found in Spain, he also experienced a deep disillusionment. When he first arrived in Barcelona there was, as he says, "Above all . . . a belief in the revolution and the future, a feeling of having suddenly emerged into an era of equality and freedom. Human beings were trying to behave as human beings and not as cogs in the capitalist machine."[21] The Spanish workingman, he discovered, had the same qualities as his English counterpart, those of honesty, loyalty, and generosity. With the common man in control, Orwell caught a glimpse, which he always remembered, of a society without tyranny and subterfuge. The idea of socialism, consequently, lost the characteristics of a vague dream and became an actuality. But when he returned to Barcelona from the front in April, the revolution had been betrayed into the hands of the bourgeois and the Russian Communist party. The realization that Moscow, fearing the alienation of England and France in the European power struggle, did not want a socialistic state in Spain finally demonstrated to him that international communism was no more than a reactionary force and could not be trusted with the future.

The revolution's failure did not, however, convince Orwell that socialism was merely an ideal and bound to be perverted. Certainly he left Spain embittered and in doubt about the immediate future. But he always retained the vision, symbolized by the Italian militiaman, of the just society. At the end of the account he writes: "This war, in which I played so ineffectual a part, has left me with memories that are mostly evil, and yet I do not wish that I had missed it. When you have had a glimpse of such a disaster as this . . . the result is not necessarily disillusionment and cynicism. Curiously enough the whole experience has left me with not less but more belief in the decency of human beings" (p. 247). His insight is analogous to that which he had immediately after he was seriously wounded. He was outraged about the absurdity of being "bumped off" in some obscure trench, because, as he says, it would mean "having to leave this world which, when all is said and done, suits me so well" (p. 200). Although Orwell returned to England very close to despair about the direction of history, he also came back to write a "homage" to man.

After *Homage to Catalonia* his thought fluctuates between despair and hope for the immediate future. On one side of the dialectic, for example, there is *Coming Up For Air*, "Inside the Whale," *Animal Farm*, and *Nineteen Eighty-Four*, while, on the other, there is *The Lion and the Unicorn*, "Looking Back on the Spanish War," and *The English People*. At last, he believed neither in utopia, nor in the ultimate annihilation of man. If anything, he learned in Spain that it is not a question of either/or. He acquired what Philip Rieff calls the "post-liberal imagination," which rejects naïve optimism for the "new temper of acceptance."[22] In other words, Orwell asserted neither perfectibility nor absolute corruption but believed that, despite the disintegration of civilization, there remained a vital morality in the common man; further, he felt that this energy might be marshalled into a political force which could defy totalitarianism and effect an extension of freedom and happiness. Writing in the *Tribune* in 1943, he says,

> The real answer is to dissociate Socialism from Utopianism. Nearly all neo-pessimist apologetics consist in putting up a man of straw and knocking him down again. The man of straw is called Human Perfectibility. Socialists are accused of believing that Society can be— and indeed, after the establishment of Socialism will be—completely perfect; also that progress is *inevitable*. . . .
> The answer, which ought to be uttered more loudly than it usually is, is that Socialism is not perfectionistic, perhaps not even hedonistic. Socialists don't claim to be able to make the world perfect: they claim to be able to make it better.[23]

This is the essence, as Laurence Brander recognizes, of Orwell's political thought: a faith in the possibility of society, tempered by fact and necessity.[24]

IV

Coming Up For Air, his fourth novel, published the year the war began in Europe, clearly exemplifies Orwell's feeling of hopelessness in the face of the approaching conflict. Before he even started the novel he wrote Cyril Connolly: "This bloody mess-up in Europe has got me so that I really can't write anything. . . . It seems to me we might as well all pack our bags for the concentration camp."[25] The fatalism expressed here earmarks his writings in 1939 and 1940 and can be seen most clearly in "Inside the Whale," written during the autumn of 1939.[26] Throughout the war he periodically reverted to a kind of despair, evident in his diary.[27] But beginning in 1941 with *The Lion and the Unicorn*, a brighter attitude develops, occasioned by certain signs, such as the blurring of class distinctions, which Orwell interpreted—quite wrongly he later admitted—as pointing to the advent of a British socialist state. Even in *Coming Up For Air* the prospects of cataclysm are muted by George Bowling's humor and joy in life. The epigraph to the novel is taken from a popular song: "He's dead, but he won't lie down."

But more significantly Orwell articulates a central aspect of his socialism in this novel. Up to this point, as I have mentioned, he had based his politics on a combination of working- and middle-class virtues, guided by the intellectual who had maintained his roots. To a great extent, he seems to have realized that this unity was vulnerable to certain world forces at the end of the thirties. The modern world, characterized by collapsing boundaries and national cultures, threatened to obliterate individuality and class mores. Constitutional strength and instinctual morality, in view of the continual centralization of power, might very well be inadequate. Thus, he saw the necessity of preserving racial memory, the idea of the past as a means of judging and ordering the present. Specifically, he looked to the late Victorian and Edwardian period as a time of relative peace which had succeeded in creating a community in which the person was offered an identity and direction. At that time society had answered the question of man's purpose and had provided economic security as well. And, importantly, Orwell believed that the working, middle class had then given meaning to human destiny "independent of heaven and hell." Even though these people did not know their order was about to crumble with World War I, they had, as George Bowling says,

> a feeling of continuity. All of them knew they'd got to die, and I suppose a few of them knew they were going to go bankrupt, but what they didn't know was that the order of things could change. Whatever might happen to themselves, things would go on as they'd known them. I don't believe it made very much difference that what's called religious belief was still prevalent in those days. . . . But I've never met anyone who gave me the impression of really believing in a future life. . . . But it's precisely in a settled period, a period when civilisation seems to stand on its four legs like an elephant, that such things as a future life don't matter. It's easy enough to die if the things you care about are going to survive. You've had your life, you're getting tired, it's time to go underground—that's how people used to see it. Individually they were finished, but their way of life would continue. Their good and evil would remain good and evil.[28]

Orwell's attitude toward tradition was not, then, idealistic, like Flory's; he viewed it, rather, like George Bowling and Winston Smith, as a useful moral touchstone for the political, critical intellect. "Reverence for the past," according to Jerome Thale, "becomes in Orwell not a counsel of perfection but the condition on which human life can continue. He feels acutely the implications of a pattern we all recognize: that as traditional values and institutions have lost their power, individuality has become more precious, and at the same time technological advances have increased the political threat to individuality."[29] Moreover, as with T. S. Eliot, Orwell's idea of the past provided him with a sense of continuity and a release from the oppression of the present.

Like Dorothy Hare, George Bowling, however, ends in disillusionment. His excursion to Lower Binfield, an outright attempt to recapture the past, culminates in the crumbling of his hope that something remains untouched by the present. At the beginning of the novel, he feels himself to be "the only person awake in a city of sleep-walkers" and that everyone is "on the burning deck and nobody knows it except me" (p. 29). Seeking some reassurance and, perhaps, an alternative in the country of his childhood, he returns, looking—as he puts it—for "air." Everything, of course, has changed, and symbolically, his secret fishing hole has been filled with garbage. Ironically, Bowling realizes that it is really he who is the "ghost," a remnant of a dead culture, holding on to values no one else recognizes. But rather than surrender his idea of life and accept contemporary civilization, he welcomes the role of spectre. He says, "By God! . . . if I'm a ghost, I'll be a ghost! I'll walk. I'll haunt the old places. And maybe I can work a bit of black magic on some of these bastards who've stolen my home town from me"

(p. 199). Even though his "haunting" is unsuccessful, Bowling does retain his memory and, importantly, uses it to judge the present and to interpret the indications of the future.

George Bowling characterizes, finally, Orwell's idea of socialism; that is, he represents the traditional culture of the English common people in whom Orwell invests his hope for socialism. With his roots in the working classes, Bowling has managed to exist in the present, unlike the classical scholar Porteous, and yet to evaluate it. He comprehends his own time because of his knowledge of the past and his class origins, and also because he has acquired through his own efforts an idea of literature and history. He possesses, consequently, the capability to survive—"he won't lie down"—as well as to understand. Despite the atmosphere of imminent destruction which Orwell creates in this novel, he also depicts a man who is able to maintain his integrity in the midst of his civilization's deterioration. Two years later in the long essay *The Lion and the Unicorn: Socialism and the English Genius*, he generalizes Bowling's qualities in his most comprehensive description of socialism.

Written during the blitz, *The Lion and the Unicorn*, although a profession of belief in the future of England and socialism, begins with a sense of total upheaval and moral void: The ethic of power has emerged unchallenged and the absorption of the individual conscience by the state has been accomplished —liberal society has obviously and finally floundered. In the face of the apparent victory of the totalitarian mind, Orwell proposes that civilization, and particularly the British, can still survive and eventually prevail. Basically, he demands two prerequisites for the revolution which can turn society away from its present direction: the preservation of English culture along with the creation of a homogeneous society.

This essay is, then, a restatement of his beliefs which evolved during the previous decade. Or to put it another way, it stands as a culmination of his political search. The political faith he articulates here remains substantially the same until his death. True, he did have doubts during the next nine years concerning the possible realization of socialism, but he never questioned the validity of his ideas. From the beginning of the forties, his political criticism proceeds from the same moral assumptions and from a sense of conviction and assuredness which he lacked before. Toward the end of his life, however, he saw that socialism would be more difficult to achieve and would take longer to attain than he imagined in 1941.

The virtue of *The Lion and the Unicorn* consists in the fact that it is a gathering and ordering of ideas which one finds in his previous work but which never appeared so succinctly nor completely framed. For example, the English common culture, which forms the basic bulwark against the modern state in Orwell's ideology but which tended to be a vague concept in his previous writings, is described in detail. In the main, the characteristics of the culture are an innate resistance to regimentation and uniformity, a horror of power worship, and a hatred of militarism, together with a deeply ingrained moral sense. The culture's uniqueness lay in its combination of an insistence on the individual's worth, balanced by a respect for law. Such concepts as justice, liberty, and objective truth, always a part of the tradition, had remained viable beliefs even in the twentieth century. More importantly, the people felt these ideas were superior to the state or any individual.

The chief problem facing Orwell and socialism was how to convert the common culture into a workable political program. In brief, how were the people to be brought to power? Because of the rigid class system they had remained submerged in the society, dominated by a corrupt ruling class and betrayed by the intelligentsia. Here he traces the failure of the educated to their separation from the common culture. Lured by Russian communism, the British intellectuals directed their energy for the most part against their country between the two wars. Instead of a positive, constructive force, they were, in Orwell's view, merely carping and negative. He suggests that "If the English people suffered for several years a real weakening of morale, so that the Fascist nations judged that they were 'decadent' and that it was safe to plunge into war, the intellectual sabotage from the Left was partly responsible."[30] In "Wells, Hitler and the World State," he goes so far as to say, "For the last twenty years the main object of English left-wing intellectuals has been to break this feeling [patriotism] down, and if they had succeeded, we might be watching the SS men patrolling the London streets at this moment."[31]

But despite the difficulties of transferring power to the common people and the ominous threat of fascism, English socialism, Orwell thought, was imminent. All depended on winning the war. Victory, conversely, rested on the creation of socialism. These beliefs, it seems clear to me, developed out of his experiences in Spain. Apparently he forgot or refused to recognize, however, that the Republic did not lose the war because it was insufficiently socialistic but because its armies were undermanned and inferiorly equipped.

Yet during the blitz Orwell did observe a disappearance of certain class privileges, which he traced both to the unifying effect of the war effort and the gradual growth of the middle class over the preceding twenty years, a process accelerated by the war itself. In this envelopment of the working by the middle class, along with the ruling class's loss of privilege, he believed he was witnessing the beginnings of a classless society. He did not fear that the amelioration would emasculate the common culture. Even though the changes might be extensive, he asserts that "It needs some very great disaster, such as prolonged subjugation by a foreign enemy, to destroy a national culture" (p. 44). If this does not occur, he continued, "England will still be England, an everlasting animal stretching into the future and the past, and, like all living things, having the power to change out of recognition and yet remain the same" (p. 44).

At this point, I think, the motivations behind Orwell's political thought become clear. On the one side, his radicalism springs from an intense conservative impulse, while, on the other, his socialism is progressive and revolutionary. This seeming paradox is implied particularly in an important passage which concludes *The Lion and the Unicorn.* He says, "By revolution we become more ourselves, not less. There is no question of stopping short, striking a compromise, salvaging 'democracy,' standing still. Nothing ever stands still. We must add to our heritage or lose it, we must grow greater or grow less, we must go forward or backward. I believe in England, and I believe that we shall go forward" (p. 96). He was convinced that unless the structure of society was altered the vital resources, latent but always present in the culture, could not flower. England's identity, was not to be created but to be discovered through a realignment of its parts. Orwell would have assented to E. M. Forster's liberal faith and agreed with his classic statement in "What I Believe" that "Not by becoming better, but by ordering and distributing his native goodness, will Man shut up Force into its box. . . ."[32]

Ultimately, Orwell's patriotism—and all he meant by the term—which emerges fully in *The Lion and the Unicorn,* develops out of a desire to found something stable, a basis for political morality, a myth—a substitute, in short, for religion. But his desire is essentially a *preservative* instinct, a demand that the present and the future be structured upon the past, which has proved to be, at least for him, permanent and vital. Revolution was a necessity, but revolution severed from traditional wisdom and the country's culture resulted in Stalinism—in an "Animal Farm." Political change required moral direction and this need could not be fulfilled by a few, who might be tempted to change the rules if the protection of their power demanded it. The check on and the guidance of power must be derived from an established cultural heritage. This is why he rejected international socialism and turned his efforts to the creation of *English* socialism. The former always deteriorated into a tyranny because it lacked the reservoirs of a unified culture. He puts these ideas in more concrete, political terms in the essay "Fascism and Democracy":

> . . . British democracy is *not* altogether a sham, *not* simply "super-structure," . . . on the contrary it is something extremely valuable which must be preserved and extended, and, above all, must not be insulted. . . . Bourgeois Democracy is not enough, but it is very much better than Fascism, and to work against it is to saw off the branch you are sitting on. The common people know this, even if the intellectuals do not. They will cling very firmly to the "illusion" of Democracy and to the Western conception of honest and common decency. . . . Any movement that can rally the mass of the English people must have as its keynotes the democratic values which the doctrinaire Marxist writes off as "illusion" or "superstructure." Either they will produce a version of Socialism more or less in accord with their past, or they will be conquered from without, with unpredictable but certainly horrible results. Whoever tries to undermine their faith in Democracy, to chip away the moral code they derive from the Protestant centuries and the French Revolution, is not preparing power for himself, though he may be preparing it for Hitler—a process we have seen repeated so often in Europe that to mistake its nature is no longer excusable.[33]

The assurance and optimism which characterizes *The Lion and the Unicorn* did not last. As the war progressed it became evident to Orwell that he had misinterpreted the signs of 1940 and 1941. He later admitted his mistakes—with his usual candor and honesty—in the *Partisan Review:*

> I fell into the trap of assuming that "the war and the revolution are inseparable." There were excuses for this belief, but still it was a very great error. For after all we have not lost the war, unless appearances are very deceiving, and we have not introduced Socialism. Britain is moving towards a planned economy, and class distinctions tend to dwindle, but there has been no real shift of power and no increase in genuine democracy. The same people still own all the property and usurp all the best jobs.[34]

V

From 1933 to 1939 Orwell published a volume a year, while during the war he wrote only *The Lion and the Unicorn,* an essay of less than thirty thousand words, and *Animal Farm,* which came out just before the conflict in Europe ended. Although unable for various reasons to do any sustained work, he did a great deal of journalism during this time, writing an occasional "London Letter" for the *Partisan Review,* reviewing in *Time and Tide* and the London *Tribune,* a socialist weekly. In 1943 he became the literary editor of the *Tribune,* to which he regularly contributed the column "As I Please." He also worked for the BBC on propaganda broadcasts to India and was a member of the home guard. These activities in themselves are a partial explanation for his failure to produce either a novel or an extended book of journalism. But the major reason he turned to other matters was the emotional demand of the war.

In notebooks kept during 1940–41 there is evidence of acute depression. In June of 1940 he wrote, "Thinking always of my island in the Hebrides, which I suppose I shall never possess nor even see." In a wistful passage, recorded two months later, he said, "Today in Portman Square saw a fourwheeler cab, in quite good trim, with a good horse and a cabman quite of the pre- 1914 type."[35] Although he longed for peace, he never seriously considered retreating from England and, according to Julian Symons, he felt he had to stay in London during the blitz in order "to set an example."[36]

Apparently, then, it was his intense emotional and physical involvement in the war which robbed him of creative energy. We have already seen in his letter to Richard Rees in 1938, while *Coming Up For Air* was still in the planning stage, how public events inhibited his imagination. Even after the war, however, he thought social conditions were seriously affecting creativity. Reviewing *The Heart of the Matter*, he says, after finding the novel somewhat inadequate and flawed, "It is pleasant to see Mr. Greene starting up again after so long a silence, and in post-war England it is a remarkable feat for a novelist to write a novel at all."[37]

Orwell's apparent exhaustion during this time is contradicted by "Looking Back on the Spanish War," written in 1942, and *Animal Farm*. The first, embodying one of his most positive statements, echoes the

ideas of *The Lion and the Unicorn*. He restates his
feelings that the common people are the most effective weapon against fascism and concludes by pro-
claiming, "I myself believe, perhaps on insufficient
grounds, that the common man will win his fight
sooner or later, but I want it to be sooner and not
later—some time within the next hundred years, say,
and not some time within the next ten thousand."[38]
Animal Farm, his most successful attempt to unify
his political thought and artistic purpose, must also
be considered an exception to Orwell's general feeling
that his creative resources had dried up during the war.

In *Animal Farm* he suggests both a temporary or
historical meaning as well as a more general or universal one. Through the use of the beast fable he goes
beyond a critique of Russian communism and its subsequent growth and decay to describe human society
and revolutionary psychology. It is important to know
that the pigs, Old Major, Snowball, and Napoleon,
parallel Lenin, Trotsky, and Stalin, and that Animal
Farm's enemies, Pinchfield and Foxwood, represent
the forces of fascism and capitalism. It is of more
value, however, to see Orwell's final purpose. After
more than two hundred years Swift's *Gulliver's Travels*
can be enjoyed without a detailed knowledge of eighteenth century politics. One suspects Orwell's allusions
to contemporary politics in *Animal Farm* will not
draw as much of the future reader's attention as the
deeper issues.

Writing of *Gulliver's Travels*, Orwell proposed that
"the most essential thing in Swift is his inability to
believe that life—ordinary life on the solid earth, and

not some rationalized, deodorized version of it—could be made worth living. Of course, no honest person claims that happiness is now a normal condition among adult human beings; but perhaps it could be made normal, and it is upon this question that all serious political controversy really turns.[39] The question of whether happiness "could be made normal," in fact, is a very central one in discussing Orwell's work after 1945 and, particularly, in relation to *Animal Farm*. If he felt, for instance, that it was only through rapid social change that England could arrive at "happiness," does the pessimistic view of revolution which emerges from *Animal Farm* signal a reversal on his part,.a turning toward social despair? Does it indicate he lost faith in the possibilities of English socialism? I do not think so. In order to arrive at the view that he gave up his belief in a political solution near the end of his life, one would have to be guilty of a very selective reading of his postwar prose. An assertion that *Animal Farm* demonstrates his complete disillusionment concerning the efficacy of revolution and, later, that *Nineteen Eighty-Four* proves his belief in the inevitability of a slave-world is founded on a misreading of these two books and on a failure to see them in relationship to his other writings.

If, in approaching *Animal Farm*, one keeps in view Orwell's qualified proposal of revolution in *The Lion and the Unicorn*, along with the ideas found in other essays such as "Fascism and Democracy," "Arthur Koestler," and *The English People*, he will see that Orwell's politics do not substantially change after 1941. Indeed, if the satire itself is read closely, it is

clear that the animals' society disintegrates, not because it springs from revolution, but because it lacks an
established political tradition. When moral direction
fails to come from the people, authority becomes absolute power, which corrupts absolutely. This situation
on the farm allows Snowball and Napoleon to change
the commandments and regulations when it suits
them. The animals do not have a "racial" memory, nor
an idea of justice and equality, to fall back on. Consequently, when at last the "single Commandment":

ALL ANIMALS ARE EQUAL
BUT SOME ANIMALS ARE MORE EQUAL THAN OTHERS,[40]

goes up on the barn, only Benjamin, the donkey,
appears unsettled, for it is he alone who remembers
what conditions were like before and at the beginning
of the revolution. The other animals accept the new
rule as a matter of course, because they do not know
what equality is in the first place and cannot recall
another time vividly enough to evaluate their present
position.

Since the animals have no history, it can be written
at will. And since they have no collective conscience,
"truth" can be manipulated or created to meet the
situation. Therefore Snowball's heroism at the Battle
of the Cowshed can later be defined as cowardice
without social disturbance. These same conditions appear fully developed in *Nineteen Eighty-Four*—with,
however, two important differences. At Animal Farm
no one challenges the pig's authority, while in Oceania, Winston Smith sees the truth—at least for a
moment—and, furthermore, the proles continue to

survive with an inherent sense of morality and a vague
memory of the past.

Certain kinds of revolutions, then, according to
Orwell, are fated to propagate enslavement rather than
to bring about freedom and to take on the appearance
of that which they sought to eliminate. Revolution,
as such, is not evil or worthless. He did come to expect
a less rapid change to socialism and learned to be
more patient with progress. But he still looked to a
socialist revolution with hope—if a muted one. At the
same time he was composing *Animal Farm*, he criticized Arthur Koestler for viewing all political action
in the modern world as useless, for advising retreat
for the time being. He explains that at the basis of
Koestler's rejection of revolution

> lies his hedonism, which leads him to think of the
> Earthly Paradise as desirable. Perhaps, however, whether
> desirable or not, it isn't possible. Perhaps some degree
> of suffering is ineradicable from human life, perhaps
> the choice before man is always a choice of evils, per-
> haps even the aim of Socialism is not to make the world
> perfect but to make it better. All revolutions are failures,
> but they are not all the same failure.[41]

In February and March of 1945 after he finished
Animal Farm, Orwell went to France and Germany
as a correspondent for the *Observer*. To be sure, what
he found there depressed him. But, although he began
to suspect that the immediate future was to be very
bleak, he was considerably heartened by what the English people had retained in spite of the war. In another
"London Letter" written for the *Partisan Review* he
says, "Having come back from the Continent I can

see England with fresh eyes, and I see that certain things—for instance, the pacifist habit of mind, respect for freedom of speech and belief in legality—have managed to survive here while seemingly disappearing on the other side of the Channel."[42] He is almost amazed that England's civil liberties remained inviolate but does not know whether to attribute this to an "instinctive wisdom" or a state of "semi-anaesthesia" in the British people.

Even in the previous year, however, Orwell was encouraged by the continued freedom of the press during the war and the tolerance of unpopular opinions which led him to hope "that the liberal habit of mind, which thinks of truth as something outside yourself, something to be discovered, and not as something you can make up as you go along, will survive."[43] He certainly realized that war maimed the human and social spirit. He saw, on the other hand, that adversity had a way of eliciting and demonstrating human greatness. Going back through his writings, one notices that his heroes and he himself respond most humanly in extremely oppressive and threatening situations. John Flory appears at his best when he is called upon to save the other Englishmen from a native uprising; Gordon Comstock eventually comes to himself only when he reaches his lowest point; and under the stress of battle Orwell and his comrades achieve a real community in Spain.

Toward the end of 1944, then, he marveled at the English resistance to totalitarianism. He noted sadly that the social gains of 1940 had disintegrated and that the common man felt politically helpless, but added,

"In spite of all that has happened, the failure of any genuinely totalitarian outlook to gain ground among the ordinary people of this country is one of the most surprising and encouraging phenomena of the war."[44] The general election of 1945 also indicated to him that the war had not drained off the people's energy. They may have voted more for economic security than for socialism, but "As a sign of the vitality of democracy, of the power of the English-speaking peoples to get along without fuehrers, the outcome of this election is a thing to be rejoiced at, even if the men it has brought to power should utterly fail."[45]

Through their vitality and integrity, the common people at a crucial point in his life demonstrated to Orwell once again that socialism was indeed a tenable political belief. The unbreakable "crystal spirit" which he saw in the Spanish people persisted as well in the English character in the face of overwhelming attack. And so, just as he wrote *Homage to Catalonia* to praise his discovery in Spain, he composed *The English People*, a neglected essay written in 1944 and published in 1947, to reiterate his faith in the ordinary man. The essay does not reveal anything new in his thought. In fact, except for a more tentative attitude toward the possibility of socialism, it parallels almost exactly the ideas of *The Lion and the Unicorn*. Although unoriginal, the essay does assume great importance because it proves he did not lose faith in political action, nor in the people's ability to achieve a just society. As in 1941 he calls for a change in the power structure within the democratic frame, the elimination of class barriers, and the inclusion of the intellectual in the common culture. The urgency he feels is not only for England but also for the rest of the world. He suggests that England has a "special mission" to exemplify that a nation can exist without chaos or tyranny. Orwell cannot say with the assurance he did earlier that this *will* happen, but he does think that it *can*. Two years later in *Nineteen Eighty-Four* he shows what he believed would result if socialism did not happen.

* * *

Written in the harsh and bitter Hebrides on the Island of Jura and published less than a year before his death, *Nineteen Eighty-Four*, a novel of the absolute desolation of the human spirit, is yet, paradoxically, a restatement of faith. It embodies his belief, enunciated in *Homage to Catalonia*, *The Lion and the Unicorn*, and *The English People*, that the common man will survive and, perhaps, prevail. The masters of Oceania have wiped away individual freedom and integrity but have left the proles, 85 percent of the population, as a possible beginning. The Outer Party, the remnants of the middle class, have sold out to the Inner Party, or they have been eliminated. The working classes, however, have been cut out of the state, left to drift on the fringe. But almost their entire history in Western civilization is one of alienation from society's mainstream; yet the proles have persisted and even at times come to awareness and power.

As if he wished to test his belief in man, Orwell in this novel opposes the human spirit to the most destructive power he could imagine. But we misread and are led to a wrong conclusion if we view Winston

Smith as the representative of that spirit. As Smith realizes, he is doomed from the beginning because his revolt occurs in isolation, with no sense of cause. Ironically, only immediately before his arrest does he perceive a purpose for his action, a hope and reason for revolution:

> The birds sang, the proles sang, the Party did not sing. All round the world, in London and New York, in Africa and Brazil and in the mysterious lands beyond the frontiers . . . everywhere stood the same solid unconquerable figure, made monstrous by work and childbearing, toiling from birth to death and still singing. Out of those mighty loins a race of conscious beings must one day come. You were dead; theirs was the future. But you could share in that future if you kept alive the mind as they kept alive the body, and passed on the secret doctrine that two plus two makes four.[46]

Winston would not share in the future, but, as Laurence Brander observes, O'Brien's destruction of Winston's comprehension does not alter the fact that he has arrived at truth, which is a victory in itself.[47] Winston's insight demonstrates that it is still possible to perceive objective reality, and this together with the proles' existence stands as sufficient reason for hope.

Besides having retained a feeling of community and family, and a memory of the past, the proles also possess an instinctive morality. In his first diary entry, Winston records an evening at the films. He recalls a disturbance which takes place during an atrocity movie:

> then the helicopter planted a 20 kilo bomb in among them terrific flash and the boat went all to matchwood.

then there was a wonderful shot of a child's arm going
up up up right up into the air a helicopter with a
camera in its nose must have followed it up and there
was a lot of applause from the party seats but a woman
down in the prole part of the house suddenly started
kicking up a fuss and shouting they didn't oughter of
showed it in front of kids they didn't it aint right not in
front of kids it aint until the police turned her out. . . .
(pp. 12–13)

Even Winston, we notice, is susceptible to the propaganda and his enjoyment, real. Afterward, however, he
writes, "If there is hope,. . . it lies in the proles"
(p. 73), and proceeds to investigate their lives, particularly their knowledge of the past. Although he sees
that the proles have maintained the family unit and
community, he also discovers that they have only a
vague historical sense, that they cannot be depended
upon to judge the present by the past: Morality is part
of their nature rather than a system. To believe in the
proles is to accept a paradox. In view of conditions his
statement of faith, as he realizes, is one "of a mystical
truth and a palpable absurdity" (p. 86).

To assert that the future lies with the proles, on
the other hand, is not only the sole possible belief but
also, in its way, logical. For if the individual in Oceania can no longer provide or expect to offer moral
energy, a community may be able to do so. As Irving
Howe correctly observes: "In 1984 Orwell is trying to
present the kind of world in which individuality has
become obsolete and personality a crime. The whole
idea of self as something precious and inviolable is a
cultural idea, and as we understand it, a product of

the liberal era; but Orwell has imagined a world in which the self, whatever subterranean existence it manages to eke out, is no longer a significant value, not even a value to be violated."[48] People like Winston and Julia are fated because they have only the self to rely on, and in this world the self is a controllable entity. The proles may not be fully human but neither have they been isolated from one another. The middle class, or here the Outer Party, may dress alike or react in the manner of automatons, but, actually, they are cut off from and afraid of every other member. The Inner Party eliminates communication among them to avoid any collusion. This is, of course, Winston's and Julia's crime.

An absolute tyranny, as Orwell perceptively surmises, would not result in a classless society. Rather Oceania is a highly divided and stratified one. The Outer Party does not know the members of the Inner, whose members enjoy all the upper-class privileges, including servants. The rulers' purpose is obvious: If all elements of the society are isolated, hence its respective talents, their own power is protected. The separation of the middle class from the proles insures that society's intellectual, moral, and physical resources will be kept ineffectual.

The novel, as I have said, should not be taken as a satire of socialism, but as a picture of what will occur if Orwell's concept of socialism is not adopted.[49] Oceania has all the attributes of the dominant culture which he fought against in the thirties and forties. Only here they are exaggerated and pushed to their extremes. The common culture has been isolated, the historical sense perverted, and political power has

passed to the hands of the managers—those who originally had no roots in country or class. This civilization
is the exact opposite of the liberal ideal, and yet, ironically, it is, according to Orwell, the logical conclusion
of the society which liberalism brought about.[50] Liberalism's basic principle, that the individual by seeking
his own welfare produces the good of the whole, has
been bankrupted. A new concept must be added to
that of individualism: The sense of community, found
only in the working classes with their built-in orientation of and check on human power, has to become a
major political value if "1984" is to be avoided. This
is the conclusion of Orwell's politics and a faith which
he never lost.

In "Toward European Unity," an essay written in
1947 in one of his more pessimistic moods, he advises
that "Our activities as socialists only have meaning if
we assume that socialism can be established, but if we
stop to consider what probably *will* happen, then we
must admit, I think, that the chances are against us."
But he refuses to give up: "a Socialist United States
of Europe seems to me the only worth-while political
objective today. . . . I do not need to be told that the
difficulties of bringing any such thing into being are
enormous and terrifying, and I will list some of them
in a moment. But we ought not to feel that it is of
its nature impossible, or that countries so different
from one another would not voluntarily unite."[51] He
saw Russian and American hostility, imperialism, and
the Catholic Church as the main obstacles to European unity. If he were calculating the odds today, perhaps he would be less hopeful.

VI

Neither Orwell's personal nor his political odyssey ended victoriously. He did successfully create a faith to fill the vacuum he had experienced early in his life. But he never saw socialism come into being—although, of course, he did not believe it would be accomplished in his lifetime. Furthermore, he died relatively young (at forty-six) when his work was incomplete and moving in another direction. Richard Rees tells us that in January 1949, after *Nineteen Eighty-Four* was finished, Orwell was planning long essays on Conrad, Gissing, and Waugh, as well as a novel.[52] This new creative energy together with his marriage to Sonia Brownell in his last year does not seem to indicate that he was a dying man paralyzed by pessimism—as so many critics want us to believe. A sounder view, it seems to me, is of a writer and thinker who had reached a relative certainty of outlook, cut off before a period which may very well have been his most productive.

His untimely death followed the pattern of hardship and misfortune in his life. Sent off at an early age to a school he detested and troubled from childhood by a lung condition which eventually killed him, Orwell never experienced security or comfort. In fact, he seemed to look for their opposites whenever he could. He never avoided an opportunity to find out the truth of his own time. He underwent deprivation in the slums of Paris and London, near death in Spain, and the horror of the blitz. None of these experiences was necessary, for he always had a more attractive alternative. But, of course, he felt there was no other choice.

At this point in history, he believed, the writer had to become involved and take risks. Yet typical of the misfortune which entered into his life, just before he began to receive a substantial financial return after publishing *Animal Farm*, his first wife died during a minor operation. He attributed her death to a loss of strength caused by the fact that she had sacrificed her rations to the poor during the war.[53] It is unreasonable in view of the circumstances to criticize him for going to Jura after the war. A widower, he had an adopted son to care for and postwar London was not very suitable for raising a child.[54] In January 1950 he died in London, where he had begun his search for a way to survive in his own time.

Orwell's preoccupation with the political events of his time partially explains why he did not write a more comprehensive political work. But the more crucial reason for this deficiency resides in the fact that he was not a theoretician. He dreaded abstraction and disliked purely philosophical matters. At times he even seems aware of his failure to develop the implications of his politics and defends himself by pointing out that practical ends must be achieved before other problems can be approached. Regardless of the historical exigencies, Orwell's inability or unwillingness to ask philosophical questions narrows the value of his political thought. He never considered, for example, how effective the common culture, the moral foundation and whole basis of his socialism, would be if and when it merged with contemporary civilization. Would the workers be able to retain their sense of communal justice and responsibility once they had made contact with the power and money ethic? The answer is implicit in his writings: Given certain conditions, such as the cooperation and return of the intellectual to society, the common culture would be preserved and eventually become the majority culture. But Orwell's failure to frame the question in any comprehensive way indicates a serious political myopia.

Since Orwell's death the problem of whether the working classes can maintain their morality as they are granted greater material advantage and whether a classless society can be created with the common culture as a base are major literary themes. And this is one mark of his influence on contemporary British literature and thought. So far there exist no clear-cut answers. Such novels as John Braine's *Room at the Top*, David Storey's *This Sporting Life*, Kingsley Amis's *Take a Girl Like You*, and John Osborne's play *Look Back in Anger* reveal a negative experience. The heroes are either corrupted by money and greater privilege or else they find absurdity and meaninglessness in their existence. The order, love, and community which they experienced as youths cannot survive in contemporary society. In other works, like John Wain's *The Contenders* and Arnold Wesker's *Trilogy*, the working class is seen as capable of moving outside their immediate environment and keeping their integrity.

There is a third point of view, one closer to Orwell's own. For example in Alan Sillitoe's *Saturday Night and Sunday Morning* and Raymond Williams's *Second Generation* the welfare state is also seen as destructive, at least as it exists. The young, working-class heroes of these novels, however, reject contemporary values, each for his own reasons, and return to their class. In Sillitoe's novel Arthur Seaton sees the working community as a refuge from the industrial jungle, and Peter Owen, the graduate student of Williams's *Second Generation*, gives up his degree to marry a girl of his own class and to work with his father in an automobile factory. One must labor within his own community to bring about socialism, he believes, because on the outside one's values are inevitably undermined. Of all these writers, Raymond Williams is the closest to Orwell. He has faith in the possibility of a viable welfare state, if the traditional culture and the intellectual are united with it. Williams, notably, is a university don from a Welsh coal-mining town. Ultimately, Orwell and all the writers mentioned share the idea that the working community possesses superior moral and political virtues. Their major dilemma centers in creating a majority culture out of a minority one.

Another characteristic which the postwar writers and intellectuals have in common with Orwell is their willingness to remain tentative, to accept society in order to deal with it. For the most part, they do not adhere to any orthodox commitment, any closed system, believing no single ideology provides the truth. Orwell, perhaps more than anyone else, exposed for them the fallacies and dangers of Soviet communism along with the inadequacy of romantic liberalism. Positively, he demonstrated the necessity of involvement in society and the vitality of the common culture. For them he is a relevant figure, more than Eliot, Joyce, or Yeats could ever be, because he has shown in his life and work one way to live in a world that is always on the verge of disaster without recourse to religious faith. And as Philip Rieff concludes: "George Orwell's active and compassionate rejection of this world that describes the old liberal imagination, coupled with his sympathetic analysis of the new temper of acceptance that describes the post-liberal imagination, makes him the writer most worthy of attention at least for those imaginations still in process of transition. He marked the transition more clearly than any other writer of his generation."[55]

Orwell's significance will persist because he never admitted the possibility of defeat, considered alienation desirable, nor saw the "inside the whale" as anything but destructive. Rather—and this is his heroism—he said "yes" to what he called "the age of the unresolved dilemma, of the struggle which never slows down and never leads to a decision."[56]

PART TWO

ART

CHAPTER TWO

Descent and Protest:
1933-1935

I

The dominant, critical attitude of the last generation has made it difficult for us to evaluate the relationship between political thought and literature. Because of the influence of what we still inexplicably call the "new criticism," which holds at bottom that ideas are alien to literature, works with an obvious political purpose are often viewed suspiciously. Lionel Trilling has defined this attitude as part of the liberal imagination, which sees an opposition between experience and ideas and asserts that literature must involve only the former. According to Trilling, these critics miss the fact that ideas are not abstractions but have their sources in the emotions. To deny the validity of ideas as material for the novel or the poem therefore is to separate the artist from both reality and a means of structuring his work.[1]

The question of the effects of politics on art is of course a central one in any consideration of Orwell. He believed that it was impossible for a writer of his generation to avoid a social commitment. Because of the historical situation, the collapse of capitalism and the advent of fascism, the writer had a responsibility to deal with politics. It was, after all, the principal reality of his time and therefore, as he said, "Literature had to become political, because anything else would have entailed mental dishonesty."[2] Furthermore, he did not view ideas, political or otherwise, as alien to literature. On the contrary, he asserts in "Charles Dickens" that "every writer, especially every novelist, *has* a 'message,' whether he admits it or not, and the minutest details of his work are influenced by it. All art is propaganda. . . . On the other hand, not all propaganda is art."[3]

In this sense everything he wrote was propaganda. Even before he gave his allegiance to socialism, his works reveal a sociopolitical purpose. Previous to 1936, it is true, he does not advocate any particular ideology; nevertheless, *Down and Out in Paris and London, Burmese Days, A Clergyman's Daughter,* and *Keep the Aspidistra Flying* are products of alarm and disgust *vis à vis* social conditions. They are meant as protests; their purpose is to elicit something besides an aesthetic response. Obviously, a critical approach which reacts in abhorrence to any kind of "message" or is repulsed by ideas not carefully disguised as metaphor would dismiss Orwell as a polemist. The question of when the doctrinal aspect of his work impinges upon, depreciates, or destroys its artistic value has not, consequently, received adequate attention.

Orwell himself never completely worked out a satisfactory answer to the problem of judging political literature. He does suggest a standard in the essay "Why I Write," where he points out that "what I have most wanted to do throughout the past ten years is to make political writing into an art."[4] To achieve this end, the writer must find some way to reconcile his life and interests with his political responsibility. As an example of the difficulty of this task he refers to *Homage to Catalonia*, in which he tried "very hard . . . to tell the whole truth without violating my literary instincts." It is flawed, however, as he agrees, by his inclusion of a long chapter defending the Trotskyists and indicting the newspapers for their distortion of the truth. In explanation he says, "I could not have done otherwise. I happened to know, what very few people in England had been allowed to know, that innocent men were being falsely accused. If I had not been angry about that I should never have written the book."[5]

Regardless of his excuse, what remains is *Homage to Catalonia*'s lack of coherence. It is not, importantly, that Orwell treated diametrically opposed matters: His defense of the P.O.U.M. and exposé of the journalists' lies are directly related to his central aim. He fails by presenting these facts as a commentator rather than as a participant, which is the controlling point of view in the book. The sense of immediacy and involvement which forcefully convince us of his purpose are dissipated when he breaks the narrative line and begins to editorialize. Although he does not admit it, the flaw ultimately stems from a distrust of art. He obviously felt such an urgency and public responsibility to reveal the truth in this particular case that he believed dramatization would obscure the facts. This commitment results in heavy-handed propaganda.

Although Orwell never arrived at any final clarity concerning the problem, he at least implies here one means of deciding whether a work of political intent is art or propaganda. He thought that only when the writer presents his ideas as part of human experiences, shows them as having a basis in sentiment and emotion, would polemic be raised to the level of art. When character is employed merely as a vehicle for argument or situation as illustration for point of view the end is propaganda. Ideas, in fact, become most effective and, indeed, only become fully ideas when they are concretized and given an emotional dimension. This is not the same as insisting that they must appear in literature only as metaphor, myth, or symbol; they can be presented explicitly, as they are, for example, in Lionel Trilling's novel *The Middle of the Journey*. This is what Orwell suggests when he says:

> My starting point [in writing] is always a feeling of partisanship, a sense of injustice. When I sit down to write a book, I do not say to myself, "I am going to produce a work of art." I write it because there is some lie that I want to expose, some fact to which I want to draw attention, and my initial concern is to get a hearing. But I could not do the work of writing a book, or even a long magazine article, if it were not also an aesthetic experience. Anyone who cares to examine my work will

see that even when it is downright propaganda it con-
tains much that a full-time politician would consider
irrelevant. I am not able, and I do not want, completely
to abandon the world-view that I acquired in childhood.
So long as I remain alive and well I shall continue to
feel strongly about prose style, to love the surface of
the earth, and to take a pleasure in solid objects and
scraps of useless information. It is no use trying to suppress that side of myself.[6]

But it was also his idea, his political commitment,
he thought, which enabled him to produce works of
artistic worth. For as he says in concluding "Why I
Write," "looking back through my work, I see that it
is invariably where I lacked a *political* purpose that I
wrote lifeless books and was betrayed into purple passages, sentences without meaning, decorative adjectives
and humbug generally."[7]

To test the accuracy of this judgment and to gain
some knowledge of the value and significance of
Orwell's prose will now be my major concern. An
examination of how his political ideas and purpose aided and/or hindered his artistic aims should
also lead us to an understanding of the problems involved in political writing aspiring to the level of art.
Finally, an approach such as this should indicate the
influence of history on art in an age of increasing terror
and narrowing freedom.

II

Although *Down and Out in Paris and London* was
first published as a novel and is sometimes still approached as one,[8] Orwell obviously had another inten-

tion in mind. His main purpose is moral and, in the largest meaning of the word, political: He wants to reveal the condition of a certain segment of society and to suggest who is responsible. The book, however, is not free from invention. In *The Road to Wigan Pier* he admitted that a few of the incidents of *Down and Out* were created and the whole rearranged.[9] But only in the loosest sense might we take it as a novel. He does not attempt extensive development of character or plot; it is episodic, with the narrator—an undisguised Orwell—providing the principal unity. To judge *Down and Out* as a novel, then, would not only be unfair but would also tend to obscure the book's real value. If one needed a definition, one might call it a dramatic autobiography, a "form" which he employs again in *Wigan Pier* and *Homage to Catalonia*.

Down and Out is seminal in other ways as well. As in almost all of Orwell's works, the main character begins in naïveté and proceeds to knowledge, another manner of stating the theme of search. Its effectiveness stems from the fact that he portrays this movement in his protagonist. Thus for the most part he brings the reader himself to a sense of discovery. Yet the narrator's initiation into the underworld is never total. He remains the middle-class Englishman to the end; complete identity with poverty is impossible because there is always the alternative of a tutoring position in England and a friend in the background ready with a loan. Throughout the journey the narrator, we feel, is in a constant state of amazement. Continuously surprised, his curiosity never abates. Whatever he undergoes, whether two or three days without eating, working as a *plonguer*, or tramping from spike to spike, he always remains somewhat detached from the experience itself. At the end of the adventure Orwell admits, "At present I do not feel that I have seen more than the fringe of poverty;" but at least, as he says, "That is a beginning."[10]

Orwell's simplicity is seen particularly in regard to the manners, morals, and living conditions of the poor. For example, in a brief incident that takes place in a London coffee shop he indirectly satirizes his own ignorance:

> "Could I have some tea and bread and butter?" I said to the girl.
> She stared. "No butter, only marg," she said, surprised. (p. 132)

In negotiating for a permanent job in Paris, he discovers his class's sense of honor is an outmoded commodity in the jungle. Out of work and hungry, he loses a prospect because he is unwilling to lie about how long he will stay. Boris, the Russian immigrant who had found him the opportunity, berates him:

> "Idiot! Species of idiot! What's the good of my finding you a job when you go and chuck it up the next moment? How could you be such a fool as to mention the other restaurant? You'd only to promise you would work for a month."
> "It seemed more honest to say I might have to leave," I objected.
> "Honest! Honest! Who ever heard of a *plongeur* being honest? *Mon ami*"—suddenly he seized my lapel and spoke very earnestly—"*mon ami*, you have worked

here all day. You see what hotel work is like. Do you
think a *plongeur* can afford a sense of honour?" (pp.
59–60)

Orwell also learns about those who exploit the *plongeurs* and the tramps. The pawnshop owners, the hotel
managers, even the hostel operators all use and de-
humanize the outcasts.

His pilgrimage thus becomes a moral encounter in
modern society, an initiation into the knowledge of
good and evil; from this he arrives at a sense of deterioration. In fact, despite the exhilarating effect which
Bozo's and Boris's defiance and will to survive have
on Orwell, the dominant and unifying theme of the
book is one of decay. For example, our first vision of
Paris is of "a very narrow street—a ravine of tall, lep-
rous houses, lurching towards one another in queer
attitudes, as though they had all been frozen in act of
collapse" (p. 5). In London, too, everything appears
in the state of decomposition. Entering a "doss-house"
for the first time, he says a "boy led me up a rickety
unlighted staircase to a bedroom. It had a sweetish
reek of paregoric and foul linen; the windows seemed
to be tight shut, and the air was almost suffocating
at first" (p. 130).

Indeed, the principal value of *Down and Out* is the
author's creation of the experience of physical corruption. His presentation of the city reminds us of Dickens's *Our Mutual Friend*, George Moore's *Esther
Waters*, George Gissing's *New Grub Street*, and particularly, Conrad's *The Secret Agent*. It is inhuman,
monstrous, and destructive. His use of vivid detail is
not merely descriptive, but it also functions to sustain

the reader's indignation and to suggest society's spiritual condition. The portrayal has its source in Orwell's own moral horror, which was transmuted into a desire to inform and convince. His primary purpose consists in communicating a message and his avid belief in the truth of what he has seen is behind the immediacy of his vision. *Down and Out*, in fact, illustrates to a great extent how the propaganda motive can inform and strengthen the aesthetic effect.

His characterization also appears to be substantially influenced by Dickens. Paddy Jaques, Orwell's mate on the tramp, is the only one of the three major characters who might be called typical or average. Boris and Bozo, however, are eccentrics. Boris, the son of a rich man, was an officer before the revolution. A comic figure, he combines the manners of an aristocrat with the appearance of a beggar. Even though he is something of a stock character, the gentleman down on his luck (a figure, by the way, which again emerges briefly in a London doss-house and the manner in which Orwell obviously sees himself), Boris is individuated by his humor and cunning. He also assumes the role of the narrator's first mentor, teaching him the mores of the underground society and a way of survival. Paddy and Bozo complete his education in England, the first showing him how to endure physically and the second, intellectually and artistically.

A sidewalk screever, Bozo exists as an image of the independent artist. Like Boris, he has come down in the world. After an injury to his foot, he could not get a regular job and so has taken to drawing political cartoons on the pavements. He impresses Orwell with his facility with French and his reading—Zola, Shake-speare, and Swift—as well as his idea of personal and artistic integrity. For example, Bozo satirizes various politicians and parties. And as he says, " 'I'm what they call a serious screever. I don't draw in blackboard chalk like these others, I use proper colours the same as what painters use; bloody expensive they are, espe-cially the reds' " (p. 161). Later as Orwell watches him drawing, he is amazed by his knowledge of his art: "From the way he [Bozo] spoke he might have been an art critic in a picture gallery. I was astonished. I confessed that I did not know which Aldebaran was— indeed, I had never noticed that the stars [in the drawing] were of different colours" (p. 164).

But of more importance to Orwell is Bozo's attitude toward poverty. At one point the author says to him:

> "It seems to me that when you take a man's money away he's fit for nothing from that moment."
>
> "No, not necessarily. If you set yourself to it, you can live the same life, rich or poor. You can still keep on with your books and your ideas. You just got to say to yourself, 'I'm a free man in *here*'—he tapped his fore-head—and you're all right." (p. 165)

Bozo demonstrated to him the way a man and an artist might live without the middle class and their money ethic—which Orwell detested and feared. During his time in Paris and London, he was obviously look-ing for an alternative mode of living. Realizing the moral and intellectual corruption that conformity to middle-class society produced, but in doubt about the effects of poverty, Orwell saw Bozo's and Boris's way of life as an illustration of a means of maintaining integrity beyond the limits of society. Furthermore, he understood that their attitude was not simply a negation or a glorification of failure like Gordon Comstock's. For as he observes about the sidewalk screever: "He had neither fear, nor regret, nor shame, nor self-pity. He had faced his position, and made a philosophy for himself" (p. 166).

The characters in *Down and Out*, therefore, are largely counterpointed to the setting. Paris and London are presented as corrosive and debilitating cities, while the people who inhabit them, especially the ones Orwell focuses on, manage to retain their humanity and identity. In this way he achieves a dual purpose, a revelation of society's condition and the assertion that the lower classes possess the interior strength to survive. This juxtaposition is a part of all his works, even *Nineteen Eighty-Four*. The quality of the characterization also indicates that propaganda was not Orwell's sole motive; for his creations are often seen as more than victims and never presented with the sentimentality which mars, let us say, Dickens's portrait of the workingman Stephen Blackpool in *Hard Times*. Besides, the narrator is quite capable of criticizing the outcasts for their lack of gratitude and their vindictiveness.

Finally, however, if his characters are vivid because of his careful use of detail and dialogue, they are closer to caricatures than personalities. They exist almost entirely on the surface and their gestures and speech do not indicate any depth of feeling or thought. His failure in characterization substantiates his disclaimer of any thorough knowledge of poverty. But even in his later books he does not have a great deal more success in creating character. And it is only in some of his protagonists, Flory, Dorothy Hare, and Gordon Comstock, that he is able to suggest something of an interior life. This inability to create characters of depth is his major limitation as an artist, a failing he was not unaware of.

More importantly, *Down and Out* is marred by what I defined earlier as "a distrust of art." The book falls roughly into two parts, the first dealing with his experiences in Paris and the second, London. At the end of each section Orwell steps out of the role of narrator-character and comments upon and interprets the action. And so he ends the first part by saying:

> To sum up. A *plongeur* is a slave, and a wasted slave, doing stupid and largely unnecessary work. He is kept at work, ultimately, because of a vague feeling that he would be dangerous if he had leisure. And educated people, who should be on his side, acquiesce in the process, because they know nothing about him and consequently are afraid of him. I say this of the *plongeur* because it is his case I have been considering; it would apply equally to numberless other types of workers. These are only my own ideas about the basic facts of a *plongeur's* life, made without reference to immediate economic questions, and no doubt largely platitudes. I present them as a sample of the thoughts that are put into one's head by working in a hotel. (p. 121)

Not only does he fall occasionally into this rather obvious political moralizing, but he also adds an inappropriate discussion of underworld slang and language in chapter 22. Certainly it is an interesting observation and one he wanted very much to make, but he included it without regard for the narrative integrity. Later in his career he admitted in a letter to Julian Symons, "One difficulty I have never solved is that one has masses of experience which one passionately wants to write about . . . and no way of using them up except by disguising them as a novel."[11] Even though *Down and Out* is not, strictly speaking, a novel, we see in this incident an example of Orwell failing to exercise his critical judgment by introducing an experience which has no precise relevance to what he is doing.

The author's political moralizing is a flaw because it is for the most part redundant. The dramatic episodes, which take up the bulk of the book, have already carried his point and, in fact, have done it much more convincingly. Instead of a unified reworking of a personal experience designed to delineate the agony of poverty and the heroism of the poor, we are left with something of an inductive syllogism. The confusion results from Orwell's inability to solve the problem of form. As in *Homage to Catalonia* he initially realizes the greater effectiveness of character and situation, but once into the work decides a "prose gloss" is necessary. The fact that this same problem occurs not only in *Down and Out* but in several other works, including his last, *Nineteen Eighty-Four*, suggests that he had an innate suspicion of the imagination; that is, he saw it as partially inadequate when one had to cope with ideas. In political thought he preferred common sense, the straight-forward and the concrete; in his art as well, especially in those works with a pointed political purpose, he appears impatient with the dramatic. On the one hand, he did not wish to write mere polemics, while, on the other, he felt the urgency and need for facts in view of the social situation. When these contradictory impulses were unresolved, the results were often oversimplified propaganda and a lack of structural and narrative coherence.

Despite these exceptions Orwell demonstrates in his first book an ability to convey the ugliness and depression of poverty. If his characterization lacks depth and the structure is unsteady, his description is extraordinarily persuasive. His powers of observation and the use of detail to portray the substratum of the modern city make *Down and Out* more than a simple tract. Throughout the book there is an underlying moral horror, the presence of a highly sensitive conscience reacting to a diseased society. No one of Orwell's generation was able to create the experience of the city better than he.

The relatively short time he spent in the slums of Paris and London made an indelible impression on him. What he saw there recurs again and again in his prose and novels. His depiction of the proles in *Nineteen Eighty-Four*, for example, most likely derives from that time. If he had not sought out this experience, he might have been a very different writer. *Down and Out* also reveals the maturing of a social conscience which might never have emerged if he had not taken his "grand tour." In Burma he was obviously influenced by the sahib manner, although not without great misgivings as "Shooting an Elephant" indicates. Avril Dunn, his sister, testifies that he had become so used to servants in the East that he would even throw cigarettes and matches on the floor and expect others to pick them up.[12] His life as a tramp provided him with an opportunity to broaden his experience and to reassess his attitude to a system he had helped to run for five years. Ultimately his researches into the nether world of society gave him a moral purpose for his life and a subject matter for his art.

III

In his next books, *Burmese Days, A Clergyman's Daughter* and *Keep the Aspidistra Flying*, Orwell turns more toward the traditional novel. Even though all these works have a sociopolitical theme, he also appears very much concerned with structure, character, and texture. After 1936, that is after he made his commitment to socialism, he went back to the manner of *Down and Out*. For example, in *Coming Up For Air* and *Nineteen Eighty-Four*, both ostensibly in the novelistic form, he combines fictional techniques with those of the polemist.[13] Toward the end of his life he was planning to return to the kind of novel he had written during the first part of the thirties. There is, in fact, much to suggest in these early novels that he was learning how to handle the form and could have developed, had he not become involved in other matters, into a first-rate novelist. Besides his ability to create a sense of place and atmosphere, as demonstrated in *Down and Out*, he shows also that he can present character with more depth and can construct

plot. Further, his careful use and development of imagery patterns, especially in *Burmese Days*, together
with his willingness to experiment, exemplified in the
Trafalgar Square episode in *A Clergyman's Daughter*,
indicates a certain knowledge of and interest in the
possibilities of the form itself.

Of the three, *Burmese Days* is the most finely
wrought. The single impression one has of the novel
like *Down and Out* is that of exhaustion—moral,
physical, and intellectual. Every element—character,
setting, imagery, and plot—is carefully designed to
support this theme. A close scrutiny of the novel reveals that Orwell was certainly doing more than writing
a satire or an attack on British imperialism. Imperialism is the subject matter, but the author is primarily
concerned with the psychological and ethical effects
of the system, both on the English and on the Burmese. The novel opens with a feeling of suffocation
and imminent death:

> It was only half-past eight, but the month was April,
> and there was a closeness in the air, a threat of the long,
> stifling midday hours. Occasional faint breaths of wind,
> seeming cool by contrast stirred the newly drenched
> orchids that hung from the eaves. Beyond the orchids
> one could see the dusty, curved trunk of a palm tree,
> and then the blazing ultramarine sky. Up in the zenith,
> so high that it dazzled one to look at them, a few vul-
> tures circled without the quiver of a wing.[14]

The vultures appear several times, but it is the heat
which is all pervasive and sends the English scurrying
to their club for protection. But there, because of fear
and the pressure to conform, the mind and will are

strangled. The club, their only refuge from the natives and the country, is itself a trap of prescribed codes, G. K. Chesterton, and the *London News*.

Everything in Burma seems designed to drive the English, if not from the country, at any rate out of their senses. As the narrator says: "One dog had taken a dislike to Flory's house, and had settled down to bay at it systematically. Sitting on its bottom fifty yards from the gate, it let out sharp, angry yelps one to half a minute, as regularly as a clock. It would keep this up for two or three hours, until the cocks began crowing" (p. 61). In a particularly significant image Orwell implies that perhaps the imperialists' principal enemy is nature itself. As Flory and Elizabeth Lackersteen stroll into the native bazaar, the narrator notes: "By the roadside, just before you got to the jail, the fragments of a stone pagoda were littered, cracked and overthrown by the strong roots of a peepul tree. The angry carved faces of demons looked up from the grass where they had fallen. Near by another peepul tree had twined itself round a palm, uprooting it and bending it backwards in a wrestle that had lasted a decade" (p. 125). One may suppose that the jail, the central symbol of British power and authority, will be soon under attack.

If the English wilt in an alien environment, they do so more because of an internal than an external cause. After fifteen years in Burma, Flory has fallen out of boredom into an existence filled with Burmese whores and whiskey. The rest of them—Westfield, Lackersteen, Ellis, Maxwell, and Macgregor—are merely shadows, although savage and destructive ones. Their

shadowy quality, even though suggestive of their na-
tures, is, in fact, a weakness in the novel. They tend
to merge into one character that is typical of the sahibs
whom Orwell hated. Mrs. Lackersteen, her niece Elizabeth, and Verrall, the military policeman, are also
made to represent certain class attitudes and are not
truly individuated. Orwell, it would appear, was more
interested in taking a measure of personal revenge than
in creating character.

His characterization of the Burmese, on the other
hand, is a good deal more successful. U Po Kyin, the
Sub-divisional Magistrate of Kyaukata, Doctor Veraswami, and Ma Hla May, Flory's mistress, are much
more imaginatively conceived than any of the English.
They all have been corrupted, like their rulers, by imperialism. But to his credit, Orwell does not view them
sentimentally—as Flory does—as noble savages spoiled
by civilization. Each of them welcomes imperialism
for his own purposes: U Po Kyin as an opportunity
for wealth and power, Veraswami as a chance to rise
above his own people, whom he sees as inferior, and
Ma Hla May as a way to get her own little flower shop.

U Po Kyin, who has gradually won promotion in the
system through blackmail and an acute understanding of English hypocrisy, is an evil, obese man and yet
strangely attractive. At one point he is described: "Un-
blinking, rather like a great porcelain idol, U Po Kyin
gazed out into the fierce sunlight. He was a man of
fifty, so fat that for years he had not risen from his
chair without help, and yet shapely and even beautiful in his grossness; for the Burmese do not sag and
bulge like white men, but grow fat symmetrically, like

fruits swelling" (p. 5). Like Burma, itself, which is
both beautiful and destructive—a combination of vultures and orchids—the magistrate is a character assas-
sin who is yet appealing, unlike the foreigners, in the
bluntness of his intentions. Because he does compre-
hend the vulnerability of the British and sees through
their pose as humanitarians, he easily achieves his aim.
By sending Ma Hla May to demand compensation
from Flory while he is in church, he forces the others
to ostracize Flory. Everyone knows, even Elizabeth,
about his mistress, but when they are made to admit
it publicly, the code has to be invoked. Therefore,
Veraswami, since he is Flory's close friend, loses face
and the opportunity for membership in the British
club. U Po Kyin is then elected.

A toady who abases himself before the English,
Veraswami stands as the most clearly realized minor
character in the novel. Like Francis, the Eurasian
policeman in the brilliant sketch "A Hanging," the
doctor betrays his own people in hope of recognition
from the Europeans. When Flory criticizes his own
countrymen's hypocrisy, Veraswami protests: "'And
consider how noble a type iss the English gentleman!
Their glorious loyalty to one another! The public
school spirit! Even those of them whose manner iss
unfortunate—some Englishmen are arrogant, I con-
cede—have the great, sterling qualities that we Orien-
tals lack. Beneath their rough exterior, their hearts are
of gold'" (p. 38). He is, of course, simply parroting
the gospel of racial superiority preached at the club
and it sickens his friend. Both Veraswami and Flory,
in view of their ideas and attitudes, are isolated from

their own races, yet, ironically, also separated from one another. Imperialism never unifies but always separates man from man. It is particularly the characterization of Veraswami, nevertheless, which indicates Orwell's developing skill. First of all, he never interferes with the presentation; but of more importance is that the doctor, whose obsequiousness is certainly nauseating, is still dramatized as a sincere man with whom we can sympathize. Orwell has not created stock character but a person whose mind has been tyrannized by an inhuman system.

Finally, Ma Hla May, although she appears infrequently, is a significant and vivid character. Like U Po Kyin she understands—if only instinctively—the weakness and the double standard of the English, especially of Flory. Childlike, she is greedy and self-seeking but also nearly diabolical in her ability to manipulate her lover. Orwell does not offer the saccharine image of the prostitute debased by the capitalists, which might be expected from a polemist, but a woman who knows her power and enjoys it. Thus, she sheds light on one of the major themes of the novel: The tyrant —Flory has purchased her from her parents for three hundred rupees—ultimately becomes the tyrannized.

The portrait of Flory does present some difficulties. The major problem centers in the question of the author's attitude toward him. For the most part he views him ironically, while on occasion he identifies with him, suggesting that Orwell had not gained sufficient distance from the experience itself. Consequently, a question arises concerning Flory's suicide. Is it merely a gesture of a deluded, sentimental, and morally exhausted man who cannot bring himself to live without the acceptance of his own effete class? Or is his suicide an act of defiance, almost heroic in nature? I believe the first suggestion is the more plausible. If not, how is one to explain Flory's idea of Elizabeth as a salvation? From the first she is obviously one of the others, loving destruction, hating the Burmese, and desiring to emulate her aunt.

And yet at times Orwell seems to align himself with Flory's self-pity and unthinking platitudes on imperialism. Early in the novel, for example, he is walking through the jungle and spies an Imperial pigeon which

> rocked itself backwards and forwards on the bough, swelling out its breast feathers and laying its coralline beak upon them. A pang went through Flory. Alone, alone, the bitterness of being alone! So often like this, in lonely places in the forest, he would come upon something—bird, flower, tree—beautiful beyond all words, if there had been a soul with whom to share it. Beauty is meaningless until it is shared. (p. 57)

Besides the fact that Orwell is too blatantly plotting here—the walk takes place immediately before Elizabeth arrives—this is maudlin and embarrassing prose. It was probably passages such as this—and there are a few others in the novel—which he called "humbug" in "Why I Write" because the thought lacked political purpose. What remains, then, is an inconsistency in tone; to be sure the dominant one is of ironical disgust with Flory's self-deception and weakness and more so with the system which can enervate to such a degree, but Orwell's failure to maintain the irony confuses the characterization of Flory.

In the novel Flory serves as a bridge, even though a tenuous one, between the two cultures. Before his death he was able to stop a native riot without bloodshed and approached the point of getting Veraswami admitted to the club. Apparently some kind of fruitful political action is possible in Kyaukata, but with his death and the disgrace of the doctor all hope drains away. *Burmese Days* is, therefore, a darkly pessimistic novel. Any kind of enlightened thought, on the part of either the British or the Burmese, is fated because of the establishment's strength and the corruption of officials like U Po Kyin. A stronger man than Flory might have been more effective, but Orwell seems to suggest that anyone who spends sufficient time in Burma is eventually rendered impotent.

About the only solace Flory can find in Burma resides in nature and this is only momentary satisfaction. As the novel's first paragraph suggests, nature is paradoxical; the orchids stand against the oppressive climate and the vultures. For Flory his walks are both a balm and a purgative. Feeling dirty and debased after sleeping with Ma Hla May, he goes into the jungle where while bathing he marvels at the Imperial pigeon. And as the narrator says: "He was happy and at peace after the walk and the clear water. It was cooler now, except for patches of heat lingering under the thicker trees, and the light was gentle. Bullock-cart wheels were screaming peacefully in the distance" (p. 58).

For Orwell as well as all his protagonists, nature possesses both a spiritual and a moral quality. It satisfies men's need for beauty, since it is something that

civilization cannot totally wipe away. And furthermore, like the workingman, nature has the power of
renewal and can defy progress. But Orwell was not so
romantic as to believe that nature by itself could provide sufficient moral or aesthetic energy. He knew this
is a post-Darwinian world and a basis for fascist ethics
can be found in nature too. Besides, man can, if he
wishes, all but destroy it, leaving only remnants. He
shows his understanding of this in chapter 14 of *Burmese Days*—the finest one in the novel—in which
Elizabeth Lackersteen's true character is revealed.
Flory takes her hunting, and although she has never
handled a rifle before, she exhibits a rare ability. Just
touching the weapon, furthermore, gives her a sexual
thrill, a feeling akin to Ellis's desire to hang natives.
The creative impulse has been cut out of the English;
their only pleasure comes in eliminating, especially
that which they cannot control or which is more beautiful than they. Ironically, Elizabeth brings down an
Imperial pigeon, a bird which gave Flory so much
peace earlier. A beater places it in her hand:

> She could hardly give it up, the feel of it so ravished
> her. She could have kissed it, hugged it to her breast.
> All the men, Flory and Ko S'la and the beaters, smiled
> at one another to see her fondling the dead bird. Re-
> luctantly, she gave it to Ko S'la to put in the bag. She
> was conscious of an extraordinary desire to fling her
> arms round Flory's neck and kiss him; and in some way
> it was the killing of the pigeon that made her feel this.
> (p. 167)

It is only at this time, significantly, that Elizabeth
and Flory come close together. Speaking of art and

poetry only drives them apart; but when he tells her of shooting and they stand over dead bodies, they can commune. The hunt is one of the high points in Orwell's art and provides a profound insight into the effects of the tyrant mentality on human relationships. Here, like Christopher Isherwood in *Berlin Stories*, he dramatizes the perversion of the sexual instinct in a totalitarian atmosphere.

With the exception, then, of a certain thinness in his depiction of the English and ambiguity in the characterization of Flory, Orwell contributed in *Burmese Days* a vivid experience of imperialism. Although in no way as accomplished as E. M. Forster's *A Passage to India* or as profound as Conrad's *Heart of Darkness*, it is an impressive novel. Like Forster he does not treat imperialism in the abstract but rather focuses on the inadequacy of human relationships under the system. Orwell's five years as a policeman enabled him to treat the political situation as more than a social problem, something that he was not quite proficient to do in *Down and Out*. It is clear, however, that the most persuasive parts of the novel are informed by his outrage. On the other hand, Flory's feelings of loneliness and self-pity, not as pointedly connected with the political theme, are the least convincing.

As far as plot is concerned, Orwell does at times interfere. Just as Flory is to ask Elizabeth to marry him, an earthquake occurs; in much the same way, while he prepares to cast a vote that will insure Veraswami's membership, the natives attack the club. Aside from these manipulations the narrative proceeds logically. Like many young novelists, Orwell frequently mis·

handles autobiographical experience and overmanages his plot. He does escape many of the hazards of the autobiographical by making Flory older than he himself was at the time. And by centering much of his attention outside the main character and on a second line of action, he avoids excessive introspection, which he was not apparently capable of treating anyway. In many ways *Burmese Days* stands as one of Orwell's most satisfying books. While in his mature works he does not fall into the trite emotions and phrases that occasionally crop up here (e.g. "her knees were knocking like castanets" and "her shattered brain looked like red velvet") and the narrative is more deftly controlled, subsequent books lack its intensity and passion. Even *Nineteen Eighty-Four*, for all its terror, does not communicate the indignation of *Burmese Days*.

IV

A *Clergyman's Daughter* is a novel Orwell regretted, sought to suppress by buying and destroying copies, and refused to have reprinted during his life. Although his objections are understandable, parts of it are among his best writing. The first third, which takes place in Knype Hill, Suffolk, before Dorothy Hare loses her memory, and the second chapter, dealing with hop-picking in Kent, contain finely observed and convincing detail. Perhaps he disliked the novel for the same reason he did not include "Inside the Whale" in *Critical Essays:* It presents existence as almost meaningless and hopeless. If *Burmese Days* shows life to be impossible under imperialism, *A Clergyman's Daughter* depicts it as nearly pointless. After his commitment to socialism he evidently changed his mind, and even though on occasion he experienced a species of despair, he finally posited the value and possibility of human life. In the chapter dealing with Dorothy's teaching, furthermore, he brutally parodied the lower middle class for their ignorance and narrow-mindedness. In this matter, too, he altered his point of view, as we will see in *Keep the Aspidistra Flying.*

Approached solely as a novel, *A Clergyman's Daughter* remains his weakest performance. Primarily, it lacks a central and controlling idea. Rather than a solidly based criticism, his targets range from the Anglican church and the clergy, working conditions among the hop-pickers, and the monstrosity of London to the private-school "racket." This lack of focus is particularly reflected in the novel's loose structure. Dorothy's amnesia is contrived and unconvincing despite the narrator's explanation that "the thing that had happened to her was commonplace enough—almost every week one reads in the newspapers of a similar case" (p. 105). It becomes an excuse for a picaresque treatment of Orwell's own experiences and various social abuses he wishes to expose. The chapter treating the school in Southbridge, for example, which takes up a fourth of the novel, is too long and repetitious. The Trafalgar Square episode, an impressionistic experiment indicating that he had read James Joyce and Virginia Woolf, fails because it so clearly clashes with the dominant, naturalistic technique. Ostensibly a Walpurgisnacht, it is a rigged and artificial attempt to compress the novel.

The characters are too much like satiric types, too farcical, for a novel of serious intent. Reverend Hare, the snobbish minister; Mr. Warburton, the country gentleman preying on virginity; Mrs. Semprell, the town gossip; Victor Stone, the earnest reformer seeking to bring the church closer to Rome; Mrs. Creevy, a tyrannical schoolmistress, and even Dorothy herself at times are all thin metaphors for certain attitudes. Only Nobby, Flo, and Charlie, the three Cockneys who take Dorothy to Kent, are presented with any uniqueness, and they appear only briefly. The lack of a disciplined structure and character depth seems to indicate that Orwell simply was not totally decided about his intentions. In many ways it is a peevish novel informed by immature cynicism—it could have been written by Gordon Comstock before his marriage. *A Clergyman's Daughter*, we recall, was his third book in less than three years, which may also account for its formlessness and superficiality.

And yet several parts of the novel are strikingly effective. Previously Orwell revealed an aptitude for handling the seamy aspects of existence and in the opening chapter where he describes Dorothy's wooden life, he demonstrates his ability once again. As in Paris, London, and Burma the rot has begun to set in. In the church—that of St. Athelstan, king of England in the tenth century—and in the few remaining parishoners the decay is evident. More entrenched in habit than Christianity, the church is literally falling apart. Only Dorothy with her visits to the poor extends the church's work beyond the sanctuary. Her father cannot be bothered with his duties and at one point complains when a workingman wants his sick child baptized: " 'Send Porter about his business and tell him I'll be round at his house at twelve o'clock. I really cannot think why it is that the lower classes always seem to choose mealtimes to come pestering one . . .' " (p. 29). Even though this is an exaggerated parody, his answer suggests what has emptied the churches: Religion is a class affair.

Dorothy tries to compensate for her father's attitude, but her attempts are futile, since in actuality she has no faith and the church is already dead. After her morning ritual of rising early and taking cold bath, which she detests, she attends the service, where she and Mrs. Mayfill are the only communicants. Mrs. Mayfill, old and dying, is described as having a "bloodless face" and a "mouth [which] was surprisingly large, loose and wet. The under lip, pendulous with age, slobbered forward, exposing a strip of gum and a row of false teeth as yellow as the keys of an old piano. On the upper lip was a fringe of dark, dewy moustache" (p. 14). Alarmed at the disgust she feels at the prospect of taking the chalice after the woman, Dorothy punishes herself by driving a pin into her arm a practice she follows after every uncharitable thought. This is a world of grotesques, of people whose instincts and values are warped and distorted. Symbolically, outside the rectory Dorothy encounters "silly Jack, the town idiot, a third grade moron with a triangular scarlet face like a strawberry, . . . loitering, vacantly flogging the gatepost with a hazel switch" (p. 55).

It is not until after Dorothy recovers consciousness in London that she gains an idea of self, and only in Kent does she experience for the first time a joy in life. Picking hops with Nobby and the others provides her with both pleasure and a sense of community, neither of which she has ever known as a clergyman's daughter:

> Looking back, afterwards, upon her interlude of hop-picking, it was always the afternoons that Dorothy remembered. Those long, laborious hours in the strong sunlight, in the sound of forty voices singing, in the smell of hops and wood smoke, had a quality peculiar and unforgettable. As the afternoon wore on you grew almost too tired to stand, and the small green hop lice got into your hair and into your ears and worried you, and your hands, from the sulphurous juice, were as black as a negro's except where they were bleeding. Yet you were happy, with an unreasonable happiness. The work took hold of you and absorbed you. It was stupid work, mechanical, exhausting and every day more painful to the hands, and yet you never wearied of it; when the weather was fine and the hops were good you had the feeling that you could go on picking for ever and for ever. It gave you a physical joy, a warm satisfied feeling inside you, to stand there hour after hour, tearing off the heavy clusters and watching the pale green pile grow higher and higher in your bin, every bushel another two-pence in your pocket. The sun burned down upon you, baking you brown, and the bitter, never-palling scent, like a wind from oceans of cool beer, flowed into your nostrils and refreshed you. (pp. 126–127)

Later, after Nobby has been arrested, only the kindness and generosity of the other pickers keeps Dorothy from going hungry. And when she returns to Knype Hill she retains the saving idea of work learned from her comrades.

But, curiously, her experience of a vital community fades completely from her mind. At the end she is absolutely and irrevocably alone. Orwell does not suggest that Dorothy has overlooked anything in her search for a solution and so it would seem he too forgot the lyrical celebration of the workers. Thus again the novel seems fragmented, for Orwell does not pull Dorothy's experience into any coherent whole. It seems that he was under some kind of compulsion to demonstrate life as essentially purposeless and yet wanted to introduce the hop-picking episode (an experience from his own life), which does indicate that a simplified life in community can be meaningful and fulfilling.[15]

Dorothy's conclusion, finally, is in some way unconvincing. Even though she has descended into the underworld of civilization, lived among the migrant workers, in a house of prostitution and the London slums, she emerges somehow unscathed. Not only does the problem of faith fade but also any sense of pity and alarm for what she has seen disappears. Her mind as well as her body remains virginal. In her insistence on self and preservation, she withdraws from life. Toward the end of her teaching career, she realizes that "it was human companionship that she needed, and there seemed no way of getting it" (p. 278); in the end, however, she almost cheerfully goes back to her enfeebling and isolated routine as a clergyman's daughter. If Orwell had viewed her solution with irony, as he does her life in the first chapter, the whole would have been more intelligible. On the contrary, she is ultimately seen with sympathy and as heroic because she has survived. What begins as a serious criticism of middle-class values ends with a shrug implying that this is all there is. Remaining unaccounted for are the viable and satisfying days Dorothy has spent in Kent with Nobby.

* * *

A Clergyman's Daughter represents more clearly than any other work by Orwell the results of a lack of any coherent political idea. It vividly reveals his own confusion about the underlying causes of middle-class society's deterioration and the alternatives to that way of life. In *Down and Out* and *Burmese Days* he had sufficient knowledge to come to some sort of conclusion about the matter at hand—he had an idea of what was wrong which enabled him to recreate, especially in the second instance, logical and unified experiences. In the case of *A Clergyman's Daughter*, however, the inconsistent point of view, the artificial and improbable structure, and the use of parody in place of characterization indicate that he had neither an adequate knowledge of his subject matter, nor a sufficiently clear concept of purpose. He was obviously going beyond his capabilities when he made his protagonist a woman, especially a rural parson's daughter, a unique breed indeed. Furthermore, the whole subject of religion and churches was, seemingly, outside his ken.

In *Down and Out* and *Burmese Days*, on the other

hand, the flaws can be traced for the most part to artistic matter. With the exception of the prose glosses that Orwell adds to the end of each section in the first book and the superficial characterization of the British in the second, instances where the propaganda motive led him astray, the faults are those of a young novelist.

The assets of this first period in his career, nevertheless, are many. His acute sense of place and his ability to convey the condition of social and spiritual sterility stand as his primary accomplishments. Moreover, he saw and dramatized how the tyranny of class contributed to inner deterioration. Like D. H. Lawrence, with whom he can be compared on many levels, he recognized the toll which subjugation exacted in a man's sexual life, the most personal domain of the individual. Not only among the tramps in *Down and Out*, for whom sex was no longer a reality, but also among the middle class, the sexual instinct had either been bestialized, as in the case of Flory, or twisted, as with Elizabeth Lackersteen, or entirely eliminated as in Dorothy Hare. Early in his career, then, Orwell perceived that the division of society into tightly restricted elements brought about the loss of personal as well as economic and political freedom. This is the time of his bleakest outlook by far; even during the last years of the war he held out at least a hope for socialism.

At this point as an artist and a thinker he needed an intellectual, emotional, and moral framework that would provide him with an order for his insights and perceptions. His descent had been made, but for both his artistic and intellectual stance protest was no longer enough. Reviewing the first three volumes of Eliot's *The Four Quartets* in 1942, he realized that

> conscious futility is something only for the young. One cannot go on "despairing of life" into ripe old age. One cannot go on and on being "decadent," since decadence means falling and one can only be said to be falling if one is going to reach the bottom reasonably soon. Sooner or later one is obliged to adopt a positive attitude towards life and society. It would be putting it too crudely to say that every poet in our time must either die young, enter the Catholic Church, or join the Communist Party, but in fact the escape from the consciousness of futility is along those general lines. There are other deaths besides physical death, and there are other sects and creeds besides the Catholic Church and the Communist Party, but it remains true that after a certain age one must either stop writing or dedicate oneself to some purpose not wholly aesthetic.[16]

There were a number of ways Orwell could have gone. Like Aldous Huxley, with whom he has certain affinities as a satirist, he could have drifted into pacifism; or like Auden and Isherwood, he could have given up on England and found solace in America, religion, and art. He could, in short, have gone "inside the whale." But because of his experiences such a course was unlikely. He was, in fact, too much like his own conception of Dickens to make any other choice than involvement: "a man who is *generously angry* . . . . a free intelligence, a type hated with equal hatred by all the smelly little orthodoxies which are now contending for our souls."[17]

CHAPTER THREE

Socialism and Commitment: 1936-1938

I

Keep the Aspidistra Flying very clearly marks Orwell's transition from protest to commitment. Gordon Comstock, the principal character of the novel, himself undergoes a change from pessimism and negation to acceptance that is brought about through his marriage, in which he discovers meaning and fulfillment. Since the publication of the novel corresponds in time to Orwell's marriage to Eileen O'Shaughnessy, it would seem that the book is in one sense a defense and a celebration of the change in his own life. Furthermore, from a grammar-school teacher and book clerk who had published three little-known books, he became after his marriage a figure of some importance in both national and international socialism with the publication of *The Road to Wigan Pier* and *Homage to Catalonia*.

During the early thirties, it is true, his political views were generally leftist like many of the young writers of the era. As Constantine FitzGibbon says in describing the Soho district in 1934, the time of *Keep the Aspidistra Flying*: "The poor young who wanted to write or paint were . . . almost all of left-wing views. They believed that their and the world's future lay with the workers, and though they came almost entirely, like Dylan [Thomas], from the middle class, "bourgeois" was the dirtiest French word in their English dictionary. To go to the pubs, to mix with the workers, was therefore not only economically attractive but also politically virtuous."[1] Orwell, FitzGibbon says, "desperately longed for real contact with the working class." Yet much of his socialism, like that of his comrades, was simply an excuse for rebellion and a way of spiting his own class, on whom he blamed the condition of the world. It was relatively easy to live in Soho with the other middle-class rebels and complain about the Blimps and the state of the poor. It was another matter to actually leave bohemia and become involved in the political situation.

When the Spanish Civil War came along in 1936, some of the young artists did join and die for the cause. But many others, like Thomas, Isherwood, Auden, and Day Lewis, watched and cheered from the sidelines. Even before the war, in which Orwell fought and was wounded. he recognized the necessity of changing his stance as an exiled Socialist. Before his marriage, he accepted the commission of the Left

Book Club to go to northern England—far from the relative comfort of Soho—to research material for *The Road to Wigan Pier*.

At the end of *Keep the Aspidistra Flying* Gordon Comstock does not, however, pledge his allegiance to socialism. His acceptance is rather of humanity. He leaves his poisonous cynicism for a family and a job. The Soho rebels would have seen this as a "compromise," a giving in to the bourgeois world; but Orwell implies that Gordon's choice is of life over that death of the spirit which infects the self-pitying and skeptical intellectual. Perhaps it is not the best or the only way, but it is better than exile. As Ravelston, the rich Socialist editor (whose character may well have been based on Richard Rees) says to Gordon: "'After all, what do you achieve by refusing to make money? You're trying to behave as though one could stand right outside our economic system. But one can't. One's got to change the system, or one changes nothing. One can't put things right in a hole-and-corner way, if you take my meaning.'"[2] If Gordon's decision is not the ultimate answer to social decay, it is the first step toward making change possible. For Orwell, moreover, a reentry into the middle class—at least the lower part of it—was necessary because it provided one with certain personal and social values that couldn't be gained in isolation.

Nonetheless, during the writing of *Keep the Aspidistra Flying* Orwell had not reached any certainty about his attitude toward the middle class. This results, as John Wain correctly sees,[3] in a confusion of tone in the novel. More precisely, Wain recognizes a contradiction between the author's point of view at the end, where he applauds Gordon's acceptance of the middle class, and at the beginning, where he aligns himself with his protagonist's sardonic attitude. Although this conflict exists and points up Orwell's own ambivalence, it is not as clear-cut or extreme as Wain would have it. He bases his criticism primarily on the novel's epigraph, an adaptation of 1 Corinthians 13, in which Orwell substitutes the word *money,* for *charity* throughout.

Early in the novel Orwell does partially sympathize with Gordon's sneering adolescence, echoes from both *Burmese Days* and *A Clergyman's Daughter*. On the other hand, he views Comstock and his pose on the whole with bitter irony and ridicule. For example, in the first chapter he describes Gordon: "He moved on through the open doorway into the front part of the shop. In doing so, he smoothed his hair. It was an habitual movement. After all, there might be girls outside the glass door. . . . He was never quite unconscious of his small stature. When he knew that anyone was looking at him he carried himself very upright, throwing a chest, with a you-be-damned air which occasionally deceived simple people" (p. 9). Later Orwell satirizes Gordon's vanity and obsession with money as he is walking, cold and hungry, past the teashops on Charing Cross Road:

> Once the glass door of a Lyons swung open, letting out a wave of hot cake-scented air. It almost overcame him. After all, why *not* go in? You could sit there for nearly an hour. A cup of tea twopence, two buns a penny each. He had fourpence halfpenny, counting the Joey. But

no! That bloody Joey! The girl at the cash desk would titter. In a vivid vision he saw the girl at the cash desk, as she handled his threepenny-bit, grin sidelong at the girl behind the cake-counter. They'd *know* it was your last threepence. No use. Shove on. Keep moving. (p. 89)

Ironically, of course, it is the little poet-rebel who is more beset with money matters than the middle-class businessman. It is not the lack of money so much as the constant thought of it which enervates Gordon spiritually and creatively. He realizes this but cannot act on it; he thinks "How right the lower classes are! Hats off to the factory lad who with fourpence in the world puts his girl in the family way! At least he's got blood and not money in his veins" (p. 57).

Even though at times Orwell seems to share some of the same attitudes he criticizes as negative and self-defeating, especially Gordon's feelings toward the middle class and money, on the whole he recognizes his protagonist's ideas as immature and emasculating. He apparently had not succeeded in completely rooting out his own bitterness and disgust. But this inconsistent point of view is by no means a major flaw as Wain suggests. If anything the irony he uses against Gordon tends to be too sharp and, consequently, we lose a measure of sympathy which is necessary to our acceptance of him at the novel's conclusion.

Orwell underlines the fact that his protagonist in his rebellion is actually very much a man of his own effete class and family, whereas he believes he is denying them. The Comstocks, as the name suggests, are an old Victorian family, part of "the most dismal of all classes," as the narrator says, "the middle-middle class, the landless gentry" (p. 48). Gordon stands at the end of the line, the last male heir, and like the rest of the family has lost the will to survive. Since 1905, when he was born, the family has produced nothing, "only deaths." And so Gordon, striving to set himself apart from the decay, inadvertently continues the tradition, although coming to it from a different way. As the novel develops he too is seen as "dead, alive, ineffectual" and "doomed, as though by a curse, to a dismal, shabby, hole-and-corner existence" (pp. 49–50). He and his ancestors, fearing the responsibility of life, choose death in its stead.

Throughout, Orwell juxtaposes Gordon and his existence to the aspidistra, the major symbol of the novel. An ugly, sturdy plant with leathery leaves, the aspidistra was a common plant in the middle- and working-class households of the time. It is nearly indestructible, although providing little beauty. Its blooms are unobtrusive purple flowers which the housewives often sought to promote by feeding the plant tea and aspirin, much as they would treat a sick child. In the novel the plant is omnipresent and tortures Gordon with its associations of the class life he despises. Mrs. Wisebeach, his landlady, has placed one in his bed-sitting room: "It has only seven leaves and never seemed to put forth any new ones. Gordon had a sort of secret feud wth the aspidistra. Many a time he had furtively attempted to kill it—starving it of water, grinding hot cigarette-ends against its stem, even mixing salt with its earth. But the beastly things are practically immortal. In almost any circumstances they can preserve a wilting, diseased existence. Gordon stood up and deliberately wiped his kerosiny fingers on the aspidistra leaves" (p. 37).

In his Lambeth sitting room, where he moves when he eventually goes "down and out," another aspidistra withers in its pot. But in the spring after he and Rosemary Waterloo have finally made love, it comes back to life. And, ironically, on their wedding day and after their first argument, in which Rosemary insists upon a geranium for the window, Gordon goes out to buy an aspidistra. Previously, when he first decided to marry, he had thought: "The aspidistra is the tree of life" (p. 293).

Gordon's purchase of the plant, with all its implications of children, semipoverty and stolidness, is an embracing of both life and the bourgeois values. It is, in essence, a rejection of what he calls the "horrible freedom," one without roots or purpose. It is also a disclaimer of the death wish which had turned him into a grotesque. At the beginning he desires not only his own destruction but the whole world's. Walking with Ravelston and noting an advertising poster, he says:

> "The imbecility, the emptiness, the desolation! You can't look at [the poster] without thinking of French letters and machine guns. Do you know that the other day I was actually wishing war would break out? I was longing for it—praying for it, almost."
>
> "Of course, the trouble is, you see, that about half the young men in Europe are wishing the same thing."
>
> "Let's hope they are. Then perhaps it'll happen." (pp. 105–106)

Rosemary is the chief agent of his recovery. Herself a member of the lower middle class (she is one of fourteen children), she attempts to bring Gordon out of himself and his hatred. In one of the finest chapters in the novel, comparable to the one in which Gordon goes on a spree with the fifty dollars he receives from an American magazine, he and Rosemary spend a day in the country. Here Orwell dramatizes the effect of modern society on sexual relations, which he has treated so perceptively in his three previous books. Alone on a small copse they are about to make love when she pulls away in horror. He has neglected to bring a prophylactic. Later, however, after his tirade about how money has infected even love between man and woman, she consents. But at this point it is evident that it is not Rosemary's virginity or her natural fears of conception or even the lack of money which prevents intercourse. It is Gordon's own inadequacy, brought on by the worry about money. He has been thinking all along about how he will have to ask Rosemary for the fare back to London. When he tells her he is ashamed to borrow from her, she says in confusion:

> "But what's it got to do with you and me making love, anyway? I don't understand you. First you want to and then don't want to. What's money got to do with it?"
>
> "Everything."
>
> He wound her arm in his and started down the road. She would never understand. Nevertheless he had got to explain.
>
> "Don't you understand that one isn't a full human—

that one doesn't *feel* a human being—unless one's got money in one's pocket?"

"No. I think that's just silly."

"It isn't that I don't want to make love to you. I do. But I tell you I can't make love to you when I've only eightpence in my pocket. At least when you know I've only eightpence. I just can't do it. It's physically impossible." (p. 180)

Again, it is not actually the lack of money which causes Gordon's impotency but his vanity and his belief that money makes human life possible. Significantly, the theme of impotency recurs later in the novel. At the end of Gordon's spree both he and Ravelston go to a house of prostitution. Although this time because of alcohol, Gordon again is incapable of the sexual act. But even when he and Rosemary do make love, she is the aggressor and he is cast in the feminine role: "she wriggled herself on to the bed beside him, put an arm under him, pulled him towards her, covered his face with kisses. He let her do it. He did not want this to happen—it was the very thing that he least wanted" (p. 270). The whole experience is tawdry, something out of Graham Greene, and Rosemary leaves feeling "dismayed, disappointed and very cold" (p. 271).

Like Flory, Elizabeth Lackersteen, and Dorothy Hare, Gordon's whole character has been distorted by his class's attitudes. He and his family have deified money and in so doing have created the cash nexus which replaces personal relationships. In reality, no matter how he lives, he is thoroughly middle middle class until the end of the novel. It is incorrect, then, to view him as returning to his class origins; rather he adopts the values which Rosemary's family represents. At the moment of recognition, he sees that

> The lower-middle-class people . . . behind their lace curtains, with their children and their scraps of furniture and their aspidistras—they lived by the money-code, sure enough, and yet they contrived to keep their decency. The money-code as they interpreted it was not merely cynical and hoggish. They "keep themselves respectable"—kept the aspidistra flying. Besides, they were alive. They were bound up in the bundle of life. They begot children, which is what the saints and the soul-savers never by any chance do. (p. 293)

* * *

Judged as a novel *Keep the Aspidistra Flying* does not come up to *Burmese Days*, although it is a substantial improvement over *A Clergyman's Daughter*. Not as ambitious as either of his previous novels, it has only three major characters and the narrative is simple and compact. This narrowed framework, however, enables Orwell to avoid the structural flaws and the Hardy-like coincidences which appeared in the other two. Regardless of Wain's reservation, Orwell does achieve a firmer control of tone and point of view than ever before, although his ambivalence toward Gordon is similar to his lack of certainty about the character of Flory in *Burmese Days*. As in all of his writings the real asset in this novel resides in the vivid picture of squalor and the creation of an atmosphere of depression, especially in his presentation of Gordon's lonely days and nights in his garret. The unromantic realism of these scenes reminds one of Gissing's *New Grub Street*; and, in fact, Edwin Reardon resembles Gordon to such an extent that it might suggest one source of Orwell's book.

A novel like *Keep the Aspidistra Flying*, constructed as it is around one character and along a single plot line, succeeds for the most part on the strength of the protagonist's characterization. The more serious problem with Gordon, more critical than the one Wain cites, is that Orwell presents him as so foppish and infantile at times that the significance of his "conversion" is lessened. That is, he has few if any admirable qualities and, therefore, when he decides to marry and raise a family, a choice which the author obviously views as valuable and redeeming, the reader wonders if the decision is indeed worthwhile. To be blunt and uncritical, it is almost impossible to like Gordon. He is priggish, vain, and self-dramatizing; consequently, anything he does tends to be suspect. This is a result of Orwell's failure to achieve complete objectivity in his characterization. Generally speaking, he is satirizing the romantic stance of the poetaster which he had no doubt observed in Soho. But he had not gained sufficient distance from the experience when he was writing the novel. Similar to his treatment of the British in *Burmese Days*, his handling of Gordon reveals a modicum of vindictiveness. But sympathy for him is vitally necessary if one is to accept the novel's resolution. The definiteness and firmness of his resolve to marry Rosemary when she becomes pregnant does elevate him to a degree in one's estimation. But more than this, it is Rosemary's love for him which convinces the reader that there is something of merit in his character.

Rosemary, as opposed to Gordon, refuses to give in to the world and has a sense of humor which puts his dramatics into the proper perspective. A country girl, she has managed to survive in London. She like her lover is dispossessed, one of the many women who have left home and been absorbed by the advertising business. She finds herself in a predicament like that of Jenny Bunn in Kingsley Amis's *Take a Girl Like You*, who holds certain moral principles and a concept of the family which are out of place in the city. Rosemary too puts up a battle to protect her virginity, not because of any religious ideas, but because she places a value on herself. Unlike Jenny, nevertheless, she gives herself freely. She is not a figure of naïve innocence, unknowingly corrupted by society. And in the conclusion, of course, her values are triumphant.

Rosemary is the only Orwell heroine who is presented as strong, intelligent, and womanly. Dorothy Hare, wan and asexual, does survive but merely in a "hole-and-corner." Elizabeth Lackersteen is a sadistic woman, destructive and savage. Julia of *Nineteen Eighty-Four* appears as the most feminine, but she is a mindless sensualist who easily collapses when confronted by O'Brien. Rosemary resembles Elsie Waters, a girl who initiates George Bowling into sex in *Coming Up For Air*. Both are what might be called traditional women, not unassuming but neither are they hardened nor possessive. Even Elsie, though, crumbles under the advance of civilization, as George finds out in his return to Lower Binfield.

Philip Ravelston, unfortunately, is nothing more than a stick figure. Orwell uses him both as a voice of common sense and as an opportunity to satirize the rich Socialist who mouths Marx while living in guilty ease. He attempts to quiet his conscience by supporting middle-class poets like Gordon but is at bottom disgusted and embarrassed by the workingman's manners. Every once in awhile he has to sneak off to Modigliani's to regain his equilibrium. There he orders a rumpsteak and Beaujolais: "Ravelston cut [the steak] open. Lovely, its red-blue heart! In Middlesbrough the unemployed huddle in frowzy beds, bread and marg and milkless tea in their bellies. He settled down to his steak with all the shameful joy of a dog with a stolen leg of mutton" (p. 123). His characterization is unfortunate because Orwell had an opportunity to depict one of the most complex phenomena of the era and instead substituted a cliché. His portrait of Ravelston, however, does reveal his idea that class differences are real and not something that can be wiped away through wishing or through the institution of socialism.

Like *A Clergyman's Daughter*, this book can be viewed as a political novel only in the widest sense of the term. Orwell is concerned in both with the fabric of society and the relationship between it and the individual. In each he arrives at a different conclusion. He presents Dorothy Hare's final choice as heroic: An isolated existence, in light of the state of belief and civilization, is the only possible one if one is to remain human. And yet a year later he understands that this kind of decision only results in spiritual death. In the conclusion of *Keep the Aspidistra Flying,* Orwell insists upon the necessity of commitment, that society——no matter its quality of destructiveness—must be encountered. The acceptance which he urges is not simply a vague insistence that one must embrace life. It is, rather, an assertion that one must find a place—and hence an identity—in the warp and woof of society and, more particularly, in class life. The tyranny of class and the cash nexus can only be eliminated from the inside by men who possess moral roots. Romantic anarchism, Gordon's disease, breeds further dissension and separation; it is the giving up of responsibility, the exhaustion of the will, which accelerates social decay.

The final implication of the novel, like Conrad's *The Secret Agent,* is that revolution based on the obliteration of all existent moral values terminates in chaos. Orwell was to make this insight explicit in his next book, *The Road to Wigan Pier,* where he urges Socialists to cast off their eccentricities and put a stop to their canting criticism of bourgeois society. In effect he asks them to end their exile based on what he considered false socialistic principles and to become part of the working classes; "After all, we have nothing to lose," he exhorts, "but our aitches" (p. 230).

In *Keep the Aspidistra Flying,* then, we have an instance in which his social ideas provided him with a means of structuring and clarifying the experience itself. Furthermore, with the exceptions of an excessive hostility in tone toward Gordon and the insubstantial characterization of Ravelston, both examples of the propaganda motive distorting the presentation, his politics do not intrude upon the integrity of the novel. Unlike *A Clergyman's Daughter*, in which the experience appears chaotic, in this novel his imagination is directed and controlled by an idea of what causes personal disintegration and what is necessary to bring about reconstruction. In short, his nascent socialism with its insistence on the common culture as a basis for change, enables him to identify society's malaise, its sources and effects, and to propose a solution. This results, on the whole, in a coherent and unified work. His ideas are concretized and given a sense of life. As in *Burmese Days* the effects of the middle-class ethic are dramatized in personal terms, and the problem of commitment versus exile, the major theme, is handled through character and image, not as an object of a sociological study.

Without Orwell's ambivalence toward the major character his third novel might very well be one of the better antiromantic novels of the twentieth century. It seems obvious that he was working too quickly. At the time he was writing a volume a year and the faults that do emerge are the kind that have their origins in insufficient planning and consideration. In view of this, the quality of his production is remarkable. Of his four books published between 1933 and 1936, only *A Clergyman's Daughter* can be judged an outright poor performance. Yet he was not to slow his pace until the war began, when he like many others felt it impossible to create. His next two, *The Road to Wigan Pier* and *Homage to Catalonia*, were also published only a year apart and were to have some of the same flaws as his preceding work. But they were also to contain some of his very best prose and in the second case he was to do his most outstanding book.

II

By accepting the commission of the Left Book Club, Orwell provided himself with an opportunity to test as well as articulate his tentative beliefs in · socialism. No doubt he felt qualified to fulfill the request for such a book, since he had done something similar in *Down and Out*. Yet the result of his expedition was unsatisfactory. Not only did he fail to define socialism in concrete and definite terms, but *The Road to Wigan Pier* itself is not coherent. Properly speaking, it should not be judged as a book but as two separate essays which are only superficially related. For the most part, the first section is a detailed account of his experiences among the industrial working class. But the vividness and immediacy of this section are unfortunately diminished by the inclusion of statistical tables, interesting only to the social historian. The second part is mainly a record of his ideas and feelings in regard to socialism, which he concludes by defining what he believes it should be and what direction it should take. So it would appear that even though Orwell had written in *Down and Out* a work that should have prepared him to face the formal problems of one like *Wigan Pier*, he did not learn from the first book and made the same mistakes again: He could not resist the desire to comment on and analyze the dramatized experience, which was sufficient in itself.

The most effective parts, then, are those where he

narrates what he himself saw and felt: for example, his stay at Brooker's lodging house and his descent into the coal mine, one of the very best descriptions in modern literature. Like many of his works, *Wigan Pier* opens with an image of decay and disintegration:

> There were generally four of us in the bedroom, and a beastly place it was, with that defiled impermanent look of rooms that are not serving their rightful purpose. Years earlier the house had been an ordinary dwelling-house, and when the Brookers had taken it and fitted it out as a tripe-shop and lodging house, they had inherited some of the more useless pieces of furniture and had never had the energy to remove them. . . . Hanging from the ceiling there was a heavy glass chandelier on which the dust was so thick that it was like fur. And covering most of one wall there was a hideous piece of junk, something between a sideboard and a hall-stand, with lots of carving and little drawers and strips of looking-glass, and there was a once-gaudy carpet ringed by the slop-pails of years, and two gilt chairs with burst seats, and one of those old-fashioned horse-hair armchairs which you slide off when you try to sit on them. The room had been turned into a bedroom by thrusting four squalid beds in among this other wreckage. (p. 7)

Later he decides to leave the Brookers when he finds a full chamber pot under the breakfast table. But it is not merely the dirt that prompts him to depart, but, as he says, "the feeling of stagnant meaningless decay, of having got down into some subterranean place where people go creeping around and round, just like blackbeetles, in an endless muddle of slovened jobs and mean grievances" (pp. 18–19). Like the young housewife he sees from the train, the Brookers are "the characteristic by-products of the modern world" (p. 19). But even more than his landlords, who are victimizers in their own way, the woman stands as an image of industrialization:

> At the back of one of the houses a young woman was kneeling on the stones, poking a stick up the leaden waste-pipe which ran from the sink inside and which I suppose was blocked. I had time to see everything about her—her sacking apron, her clumsy clogs, her arms reddened by the cold. She looked up as the train passed, and I was almost near enough to catch her eye. She had a round pale face, the usual exhausted face of the slum girl who is twenty-five and looks forty, thanks to miscarriages and drudgery; and it wore, for the second in which I saw it, the most desolate, hopeless expression I have ever seen. It struck me then that we are mistaken when we say that "It isn't the same for them as it would be for us," and that people bred in the slums can imagine nothing but the slums. For what I saw in her face was not the ignorant suffering of an animal. She knew well enough what was happening to her—understood as well as I did how dreadful a destiny it was to be kneeling there in the bitter cold, on the slimy stones of a slum backyard, poking a stick up a foul drainpipe. (p. 20)

In "epiphanies" such as this and in the description of the excruciating and dehumanizing miner's "crawl," Orwell creates a persuasive image of the working-man's dilemma, much more convincing than any list of statistics or vitriolic polemic.

He not only found the worker degraded and de-
humanized however, but also discovered, as he did in
Down and Out, qualities of heroism, dignity, and a
basic decency. He views the miners as men of super-
human strength and endurance; and as he says, "all
of us *really* owe the comparative decency of our lives
to the poor drudges underground, blackened to the
eyes, with their throats full of coal dust, driving their
shovels forward with arms and belly muscles of steel"
(p. 36). And everywhere he goes, into homes and
mines, he is received with "extraordinary courtesy and
good nature" (p. 74). If he falls into occasional sentimentality when he details the "prosperous" working-
class household, he does succeed in creating a picture
which complements and balances the dominant bleak-
ness, and which, therefore, goes toward validating a
socialism based essentially on the English laborer's
values.

And so even if we view *Wigan Pier* as a book which
again reveals Orwell's inability to discover or create a
suitable form for his material, it should not be passed
over nor wholly condemned. Not only are there examples of his artistic abilities but there is also a long section of self-revelation, written with his own particular
candor, humor, and honesty, of special value to anyone
interested in his life and mind. Its greatest significance,
nevertheless, might be its place in his development
as an artist. For after *Wigan Pier* he achieves maturity
as a writer, manifested in his powers of objectivity and
precision. And even though he does not always manage to unite the dramatic and polemic in some of his
subsequent works, his failures in form are not so irk-

some nor blatant as they are in *Down and Out, A Clergyman's Daughter*, and *Wigan Pier*. Furthermore, in his next book, *Homage to Catalonia*, similar to *Down and Out* and *Wigan Pier* in purpose and execution, he accomplishes the task, although still imperfectly, of elevating dramatic journalism to the level of art.

* * *

The basic reason for *Homage to Catalonia's* success stems from the fact that there is a distance between the author and the first-person narrator. That is, except for those times when Orwell steps in to deliver what amounts to Trotskyite propaganda, the narrator is actually one of the dramatis personae, experiencing the war and disillusionment. Even though the author is writing from the advantage of knowledge concerning the events, in the main he does not allow his omniscience to intrude upon the narration. By electing to employ the limited narrator, he gives his major theme, the naïve man sacrificed to political expediency, a dramatic context. And further, as Emmanuel Edrich points out, he substantiates his theme by writing in a prose which with its directness and simplicity reflects the narrator's predicament.[4]

From the very first, when the narrator arrives in Barcelona, he communicates a childlike sense of wonder and amazement in what appears to be a worker's state. The handclasp of the Italian militiaman, who always remained for Orwell a symbol of the working-class spirit, and the lack of distinction in dress and manner impressed upon him the possibility of equality. Yet as he admits, "All this was queer and moving.

There was much in it that I did not understand, in some ways I did not even like it, but I recognized it immediately as a state of affairs worth fighting for" (p. 3). After this initial experience he actively resists the political complexities of the war itself. He wanted so desperately to see it simply as a class conflict that he set himself up for disillusionment.

Homage to Catalonia, in fact, might be seen as a parable of the British and American intellectual who flirted with socialism in the thirties: the young rebel who after a willful blindness to the nature of reality and Soviet communism is awakened suddenly to the fact that he is only a pawn in an international power struggle. For example, Orwell insists throughout the first part of the book that "the political side of the war bored me" (p. 60), and "at the time I could not bring myself to take [the political debate] very seriously. The inter-party feud was annoying and even disgusting, but it appeared to me as a domestic squabble" (p. 69). He is both uninterested in, and unaware of, politics. He arrives in Spain totally unprepared for the experience. And so, as with *Down and Out* and *A Clergyman's Daughter* among others of his works, *Homage to Catalonia* embodies the theme of descent, an encounter with the underlying nature of modern politics and society.

As long as Orwell remains outside of Barcelona and in the front lines with his comrades and the peasants, socialism is actual. Without the distinction of rank and the consequent discipline, even the fighting seems more human, almost a game but, of course, inefficient. At one point, like a tourist, he decides to photograph one of his own machine-gun nests. He describes the incident:

> "Don't fire," I said half-jokingly as I focused the camera.
> "Oh no, we won't fire."
> The next moment there was a frightful roar and a stream of bullets tore past my face so close that my cheek was stung by grains of cordite. It was unintentional, but the machine-gunners considered it a great joke. (p. 36)

Another time a comrade, Jaime Domenech, asks him to explain the password, *eroica*. He replies that it means the same as *valiente*. The consequences are nearly fatal. Orwell finishes the anecdote:

> A little while later he was stumbling up the trench in the darkness, and the sentry challenged him:
> "Alto! Cataluna!"
> "Valiente!" yelled Jaime, certain that he was saying the right thing.
> Bang!
> However, the sentry missed him. In this war everyone always did miss everyone else, when it was humanly possible. (p. 37)

Although the Spanish Civil War lacked the chivalry and heroism that characterized World War I before 1916 and the Battle of the Somme, it was similar in its naïve idealism. Given the experience of equality in an army without a highly rigid and mechanized character, Orwell believed that socialism would be realizable in the near future. As he comments, "the Spanish militias, while they lasted, were a sort of microcosm of a classless society. In that community where no one was on the make, where there was a shortage of everything but no privilege and no boot-licking, one got, perhaps, a crude forecast of what the opening stages of Socialism might be like. And, after all, instead of disillusioning me it deeply attracted me. The effect was to make my desire to see Socialism established much more actual than it had been before" (p. 112).

This was in Aragon, however, in the mountains, where the city and its complicated ideas could not reach. The descent to Barcelona is one into civilization, where there was "a peculiar feeling of evil in the air" (p. 209). The unfounded expectations and innocence of the militiamen cannot survive in this climate. Coming back from the front after three and a half months, "Everyone," as Orwell says, "was profoundly happy, more happy than I can convey. But when the train had rolled through Sabadell and into Barcelona, we stepped into an atmosphere that was scarcely less alien and hostile to us and our kind than if this had been Paris or London" (p. 116). Therefore John Mander is mistaken in viewing Orwell as merely a Trotskyite propagandist when he defends the P.O.U.M. against the accusations that it was betraying the revolution.[5] He was not, finally, defending an ideology but rather an emotion or experience which he had had with the militia. He may have been naïve about the political ramifications of the various parties in Barcelona, but he was not wrong about the reality of his experience. His disillusionment was in the realization that his concept of socialism was not compat-

ible with the European political situation. Spiritually
satisfying as it might be, a creed based on such fundamental human values as justice, decency, and camara-
derie was not sufficient to direct a political movement
or combat the *realpolitik* of Stalin, Hitler, Mussolini,
and Franco, who were only interested in solidifying
their positions of power; individual freedom, therefore,
had to be dispensed with. Orwell's socialism could
not survive in this situation because it was not *political* enough. During the Second World War he came
to understand that a romantic belief in the ordinary
man had to be supported by political realism; that
one would have to employ the tactics of the practical
politician, at the risk of becoming like the enemy, in
order to bring about socialism. It is a difficult lesson
to learn, but necessary if one is to mature politically.

Ultimately it is the ardency of his belief in the common man which gives *Homage to Catalonia* its power
of persuasion and life. Emotionally, at least, Orwell
had arrived at a surety of faith and allegiance—the
details were to be worked out at a later time—which
were absent from his previous work. If this same situation led him to confuse his artistic and polemic intentions, it also produced a greater clarity of idea than
ever before. It is as if his discovery of forthrightness
and simplicity in a concrete and uncommon way resulted in similar qualities in *Homage to Catalonia*.
Dramatic incidents, such as those depicting his comrades in arms, the train rides, his own wounding, and
his heroic although unsuccessful attempt to save a
colleague from the authorities, are rendered with both
a sense of love and importunity, an urgency based on
the recognition that something of great moral and

social value was being methodically destroyed by ignorance and maliciousness.

Apparently the psychic wounds he had received in Burma, Paris, and London only succeeded in bringing him to the point of exhaustion. It took the nearly fatal experience in Spain to convince him that life and his own civilization were worth having. What he realized after his wounding was the culmination of a process which had begun with his marriage and the writing of *Keep the Aspidistra Flying*, a development which brought him to see the significance of life and the necessity of remaining involved in society no matter the circumstances. Recalling his wounding and being carried off the battlefield with blood bubbling out of his mouth, he writes, "The leaves of the silver poplars which, in places, fringed our trenches brushed against my face; I thought what a good thing it was to to be alive in a world where silver poplars grow" (p. 201).

From this point until his death in 1950 he spent his time explaining, defending, and working for the vision he had gained in Spain. The events of the next twelve years made his experience appear at times like a dream of the irrevocable past, similar to George Bowling's dream of Edwardian England. But Orwell never did fall into the error of confusing ideals with ideas; through the blitz, the atomic bomb and the postwar confusion, he retained the concept of a common culture which he salvaged from the disappointment of Spain and which together with his faith in the English working class finally enabled him to create a means of evaluating experience both as a man and as an artist.

CHAPTER FOUR

Dilemma and Conclusion: 1939-1950

I

After Orwell finished *Homage to Catalonia*, he slipped into a depression occasioned by the approach of World War II and by a return of a lung ailment, complicated by the neck wound he received in Spain. At any rate, he felt unable to work on his next novel, *Coming Up For Air*. Aided by an anonymous donor,[1] he went to French Morocco with his wife in the winter of 1938–39 to recuperate. His lungs cleared up to an extent, and although *Coming Up For Air* was finished in 1939, his outlook was still close to despair as evidenced by "Inside the Whale," written in the same year. The novel, on the other hand, even though bleak in its prospect for the immediate future, is in many places highly humorous, rather uncharacteristic of his work up to this point. The drama of the novel, in fact, stems from George Bowling's insistence on his own survival in the face of almost certain disaster. To a great extent Bowling is supported by his sense of the ridiculous, his ability to see both himself and those around him as absurd. This capability springs from his idea of the past, which alienates him from the present and, consequently, allows him a means of judgment.

It is not only his humor, however, which mitigates the psychological effects of civilization and protects him from despair, but also his love of ordinary existence. Similar to Orwell's own assertion of life's value at the moment of near death in Spain, Bowling opts—no matter the circumstances—for the world:

> If I'd had a mirror I'd have looked at the whole of myself, though, as a matter of fact, I knew what I looked like already. A fat man of forty-five, in a grey herringbone suit a bit the worse for wear and a bowler hat. Wife, two kids and a house in the suburbs written all over me. Red face and boiled blue eyes. I know, you don't have to tell me. But the thing that struck me, as I gave my dental plate the once-over before slipping it back into my mouth, was that *it doesn't matter.* Even false teeth don't matter. I'm fat—yes. I look like a bookie's unsuccessful brother—yes. No woman will ever go to bed with me again unless she's paid to. I know all that. But I tell you I don't care. I don't want the women, I don't even want to be young again. I only want to be alive. And I was alive that moment when I stood looking at the primroses and the red embers under the hedge. It's a feeling inside you, a kind of peaceful feeling, and yet it's like a flame. (pp. 166–167)

Even at the end of the novel, when his myth of Lower Binfield has been exploded and he returns, now more than ever certain of war, Bowling retains his ironical attitude toward himself and insistence on survival. Having left the place of his youth forecasting doom ("I only know that if there's anything you care a curse about better say good-bye to it now, because everything you've ever known is going down, down, into the muck, with the machine-guns rattling all the time" [p. 229]), he arrives home to find that he is no longer in an apocalyptic mood:

> I say what bloody rot it was, this business that I'd wasted the last five days on. Sneaking off to Lower Binfield to try and recover the past, and then, in the car coming home, thinking a lot of prophetic baloney about the future. The future! What's the future got to do with chaps like you and me? Holding down our jobs— that's our future. As for Hilda, even when the bombs are dropping she'll still be thinking about the price of butter. (pp. 229–230)

The implication of this passage, like the entire novel, is as George Woodcock says, "Life is always defeated, because death exists. But it is always there to pose the challenge anew."[2] Like Gordon Comstock, then, "Fatty" Bowling retreats from negation to the workaday world and to his family.

In other words, Bowling has what Orwell calls in his essay "The Art of Donald McGill" "the Sancho Panza view of life"; he is the "little fat man who sees very clearly the advantages of staying alive with a whole skin."[3] In short, Bowling stands not so much as a threat (he always seeks the line of least resistance), but as a small rebellious pest to the official world. And since he is a representative of that side of human nature which Orwell sees as ultimately uncontrollable, he will get along under the worst conditions, even in an absolute tyranny. As he says after describing a totalitarian future, a picture by the way which was to become Oceania, "But the ordinary middling chaps like me will be carrying on just as usual" (p. 153).

All the rest, the Socialists, the middle class and the liberal intellectuals like Porteous are fated to be swallowed by the state. The Left, in general, as Bowling learns at the suburban meeting of the Left Book Club, have adopted the tactics and hatred of the enemy, fascism. The middle class has sold its birthright to the boss and the system and is left without any freedom, even in private. And finally the educated, who naïvely believe, like the judge in Stephen Spender's play *Trial of a Judge*, that reason will eventually triumph, are impotent against the *realpolitik* of modern civilization. Because Porteous is a man out of his time, Bowling feels a certain sympathy for and identity with him; but he also knows that no remnant can persist unless it understands the enemy or has taproots in the vital, physical existence of the past. It is this instinctual drive for life which one finds in the Italian soldier, Bowling, the donkey in *Animal Farm*, and the proles in *Nineteen Eighty-Four* that will insure their preservation against any force.

In at least one way, then, *Coming Up For Air* can be viewed as a novel in which Orwell sought to dramatize his experience of the "crystal spirit" which he had had in Spain. This autobiographical element is suggested by a letter he wrote to Julian Symons after the latter reviewed the second edition of the novel in 1948. In the letter Orwell says,

> Of course you are prefectly right about my own character intruding on the narrator. I am not a real novelist anyway, and that particular vice is inherent in writing a novel in the first person, which one should never do. One difficulty I have never solved is that one has masses of experience which one passionately wanted to write about, e.g. the part about fishing in that book, and no way of using them up except by disguising them as a novel.[4]

Here he recognizes the principal problem one has with the novel, the character of Bowling. The episodes dealing with fishing, contrary to his statement, function extremely well as a metaphor of the theme of the vital past. Besides, they are richly and imaginatively done, reminding one of the hop-picking scenes in *A Clergyman's Daughter*.

I am led to believe, nevertheless, by the somewhat contradictory aspects of Bowling's character that Orwell manipulates him in order to define a political-moral idea. Not only is Bowling the "crystal spirit" which Orwell counted on to endure totalitarianism, but also, as I have pointed out previously, he embodies all the basic elements of Orwell's socialism: He is middle class, yet deeply a part of the common culture; furthermore, Bowling is something of an intellectual, widely read and knowledgeable. More than this, one has difficulty accepting Orwell's plotting of his character development. It seems out of keeping with Bowling's common sense and intellectual development when, after returning from the army, he becomes an insurance salesman and marries Hilda, a dried-up, emotionless shrew, a daughter of an effete Anglo-Indian family. Thereafter, he is trapped in a loveless marriage with children he cannot tolerate. Not only does Orwell work inconsistently with the given of his character in order to set up a situation where the trip to Lower Binfield is conceivable but he attributes elements to Bowling which do not harmonize. For example, if Bowling is so aware of conditions, why is he so thoroughly disillusioned on his return to the country? I suspect that the entire plot structure is an elaborate device to illustrate the reason behind society's disintegration and to delineate the kind of character which will survive.

Furthermore, the whole accidental bomb incident, which is central to the novel, finally convincing Bowling that "the bad times are coming, and the streamlined men are coming too" (p. 229), seems rigged and sensational. Before the explosion he has already realized that there is no real "air" to come up for. The reaction on the part of the Air Ministry, besides, is exaggerated and unrealistic. Bowling says, "Afterwards . . . the Air Ministry sent a chap to inspect the damage, and issued a report saying that the effects of the bomb were 'disappointing'. As a matter of fact it had only killed three people . . ." (p. 226). Here Orwell is quite obviously letting his bitterness distort probability.

His handling of the minor characters also indicates that he was not so much interested in writing a novel as in illustrating certain ideas. Without exception they are shadowy and lack delineation. Hilda, Bowling's children: Billy and Lorna, Porteous, and even the characters from the past hardly exist for us. The more polemical his intention was, the less he was interested in creating minor characters or setting. Only in his first novel, *Burmese Days*, did he attempt to develop every possibility of fiction.

As in all his novels, however, there are factors in *Coming Up for Air* which survive the inadequacies of plot and characterization and which make it valuable. Besides the novel's energy of manner and the protagonist's humor, there is his recreation of Edwardian England, which takes up a third of the book and is an artistic triumph. It is one of the few incidents of any magnitude in his works which he had not directly experienced. Yet in atmosphere and detail it is equal or superior to any of his prose. Certainly Orwell saw remnants of pre-1914, lower-middle-class life even in the thirties and could sense the spirit of what it was like to be among working-class elements. To a great extent he also translated his experiences in Spain into English terms. In time and circumstances, however, he was creating out of his imagination. Even Oceania, although placed in the future, resembles London during the war. The question, of course, is not whether his description of his past is a replica of life at the turn of the century. Certainly Edwardian society does not appear as an idyllic dream. If the picture is informed with a kind of nostalgia for a culture based on a belief in continuity, dignity, and freedom, it is also rendered as brutal and unenlightened. Orwell was not only concerned with creating a sense of the past but also with dramatizing the moral and political worth of an idea which he believed existed thirty years previously and at least occasionally in the present. He succeeded in this because he presented it in believable human terms, as he did in *Homage to Catalonia*.

Both the strengths and weaknesses of *Coming Up For Air* stem directly from his time in Spain; there he had at last seen values which could endure—if only in the undergound—the impact of modern civiliza-tion. His involvement with that experience enabled him to reproduce these virtues vividly in this novel. Indeed, to look ahead for a moment, the chief strengths of his last two works have the same source. But it was also the depth of his commitment which led, as in *Homage to Catalonia*, to flaws in structure and character. His fear of the future was genuine, and immediately before World War II he fully expected that a dictatorship of one kind or another would be imposed when hostilities began. He even proposed to Herbert Read that they set up a secret press to print revolutionary and socialist pamphlets because the sup-pression of speech and press was inevitable.[5] This be-lief in the need for prompt action and defense emerges in the polemical elements in *Coming Up For Air*. Art, especially the novel, suffers during the time of great social upheaval. And this observation is nowhere more clearly demonstrated than in Orwell's work.

In light of this, it is noteworthy that he turns away from the realistic novel in his next work, *Animal Farm*, a beast allegory. And even *Nineteen Eighty-Four*, although realistic in detail, is more symbolic in nature. Indeed, his final two books can be considered on one level as dreams. *Animal Farm*, furthermore, is his most satisfying book from an aesthetic point of view. In many ways it does resemble *Coming Up For Air* in theme and manner, but with the essential difference that this time Orwell found in allegory a form suited to his purpose. The novel, it seems, did not permit him to express what he felt bound to say explicitly, but when the restrictions of that form were lifted, he felt imaginatively freer and could combine the polemic and dramatic to better advantage.[6]

II

Throughout his life Orwell had a deep affection for animals. Although he often criticized the English for showing coddling devotion to dogs and cats, he frequently wrote of animals with feeling and in the same way as D. H. Lawrence was able to empathize with them. In general he admired their ability to endure human tyranny as well as their faithfulness. In "Marrakech" he describes the Moroccan donkey:

> hardly bigger than a St Bernard dog, it carries a load which in the British Army would be considered too much for a fifteen-hands mules, and very often its pack-saddle is not taken off its back for weeks together. But what is peculiarly pitiful is that it is the most willing creature on earth, it follows its master like a dog and does not need either bridle or halter. After a dozen years of devoted work it suddenly drops dead, whereupon its master tips it into the ditch and the village dogs have torn its guts out before it is cold.[7]

He also saw in the animal realm the facility for surviving nature itself. For example, he was reassured in the spring not only by the appearance of birds, but also by the resurrection of the common toad. It gave him a special kind of pleasure to know even the ugly and unappealing could come through.

In the truest sense Orwell was a man of reverence. He venerated nature not in a shallow, romantic way, nor finally because of an attachment to preindustrial culture; rather he approached it as sacred and sacramental. Like Hardy and—again—Lawrence, he viewed any attack on nature as a denial of the sanctity of life; man's brutality toward animals, for instance, signified for him an outright negation of existence. Elizabeth Lackersteen's pleasure in killing the Imperial pigeons, analogous to Gerald Crich's subjugation of the mare in *Women in Love*, reflects a hatred of self and the world. On the other side, George Bowling's attitude toward fish indicates his vital connection with life. Domestic animals, we recall, are eliminated in Oceania.

In the last analysis, however, Orwell was awed by both animate and inanimate nature for the same reason he revered the human person. In all being he saw and rejoiced in the desperate struggle for existence against insuperable odds. He did not overlook the impulse toward death in creation; he accepted it. Yet he stressed its opposite and, like Freud, saw the instinct to survive as possessing cultural value. He would have agreed, I think, with Trilling that Freud's emphasis on biology represents

> a resistance to and a modification of the cultural omnipotence. We reflect that somewhere in the child, somewhere in the adult, there is a hard, irreducible, stubborn core of biological urgency, and biological necessity, and biological *reason*, that culture cannot reach and that

reserves the right, which sooner or later it will exercise, to judge the culture and resist and revise it. It seems to me that whenever we become aware of how entirely controlled by it we believe ourselves to be, destined and fated and foreordained by it, there must come to us a certain sense of liberation when we remember our biological selves.[8]

In fact, in viewing the animal Orwell may very well have found reason to assert the invulnerability of man. The possibility that worried him was not so much that humans might turn into animals but that the people who, like the proles, had maintained their instincts would become thoroughly civilized. Or to put it another way, one cannot afford to ignore, he argues, the unconscious morality of the clownlike dog that embarrasses the executioners in "A Hanging."

In *Animal Farm* Orwell illustrates—better than in any other work—both his affection for animals and his idea that certain civilizing influences threaten the moral dimension of the instincts; that "animals" may begin to resemble men until it is "impossible to say which [is] which" (p. 91). In light of this one can see that he makes use of the beast fable for two principal reasons: It provides a suitable vehicle for satire, and it is also thematically relevant. Animals are humorous in themselves, can serve as convenient metaphors for certain vices and virtues (pigs are greedy; donkeys, stubborn, and horses, hardworking, etc.), and finally, they can symbolize the positive, biological instincts. They are communal, loyal, and self-sacrificing. It is important to note in the satire that the animals' corruption results from contact with man or the tools

of his civilization. Not until after they win the Battle
of the Cowshed and fully assume Farmer Jones's place
does injustice begin. The pigs, Snowball and Napoleon, weaken themselves by living in the farmhouse.
And, importantly, the dogs, Bluebell, Jessie, and
Pincher, are taken from their mother at birth and put
through a form of brainwashing to turn them into
brutal killers. Mollie, the foolish and vain mare,
has been spoiled by Jones, and Moses, the conniving,
clerical raven, has learned his theology from the
outside world.

The point that Orwell makes here is not that the
bare, natural instincts are politically or socially sufficient. As George Woodcock contends, nevertheless,
he tended to believe, like the romantics, that man
possessed inherent virtues which were the foundation
for a moral life and which contemporary culture was
bent on eliminating.[9] This anarchistic aspect was, of
course, present in his thought, but it should not be
overemphasized. As I have continually stressed, he
never asserted perfectibility inside, and certainly not
outside, the social order; institutions, based on a con-
scious moral and historical sense, were required to
give the person direction and order. Indeed, if in *Animal Farm* he symbolically suggests the ethical validity
of the natural instincts, he also underlines how easily
these instincts can be perverted. And if they are never
totally obliterated—Benjamin, the donkey, survives on
the periphery—they are, as in the proles, of little political value. In a situation like Animal Farm or Oceania, however, where almost every element of existence
can be manipulated, if there is a hope it must lie in

the uncontrollable, the nonrational. Here again Orwell's relationship with Lawrence as well as Forster is apparent. Although there are important differences in emphasis among them in this matter, all three felt that especially in a highly industrial and organized society the irrational and spontaneous elements in human character must be given play.

The artistic value of *Animal Farm*, then, rests on Orwell's choice of metaphor and form. The conflict between biological instinct and civilization is succinctly mirrored in the animals' revolution against Farmer Jones. The allegorical form itself suggests the universality of the drama. The historical relevance, the fact that the author was satirizing the Soviet revolution, is, as I suggested, of comparatively minor importance. It cannot be overlooked, certainly, since it gives his major theme a definite historical validity. Even though *Animal Farm* remains as the only completely successful example of his combining of aesthetic and political intentions, it should not be assumed that it is a "sport" in his work. We have seen that all the ingredients of the satire were present in one way or another in his previous books.

Nor was his choice of form merely fortuitous. He was never totally satisfied with the novel as a way of expressing his purposes and only used the form because at the time he saw no other alternative. In "Inside the Whale," written in 1939 and later rejected because he no longer, it seems, agreed with its pessimistic spirit, he expresses doubt about the efficacy of the genre in an "atmosphere of orthodoxy." Not only did he feel that he had failed with the novel, but he also believed that the form as a whole had degenerated during the thirties and only polemics and poetry had survived with any permanent value.[10] Indeed, in the broadest sense, one might call *Animal Farm* a poem, existing as it does almost solely on the metaphorical and symbolic level. And, furthermore, much of its virtue consists in its rigid economy of expression and its clarity and simplicity of language.[11] It seems, therefore, that in selecting the allegorical form Orwell sought a means of clearly expressing his political ideas without having to deal with the requisites of the novel.

But even after his achievement in *Animal Farm* has been recognized, that as in no other work he manages to find an imaginative expression for his political purpose, there exists a sense of the book's inadequacy. More often than not it is regarded as his finest work because of the attributes discussed. And yet when one compares it to some of his other books, especially *Burmese Days, Homage to Catalonia,* and *Nineteen Eighty-Four,* which are admittedly flawed, *Animal Farm* tends to pale. Paradoxically, the reason stems from the source that insures its aesthetic goodness. For all its usefulness, the animal metaphor limits by its very nature the complexity and emotional depth of the experience. Although our sympathy and anger are aroused by the plight and fate of the animals, we never become as involved with them as we would with human characters. If the metaphor points to the human situation, it never permits the profundity of emotion that emerges, let us say, in Flory's or Winston Smith's dilemma. If we look with pity on Boxer as he is trucked to the knackers, we are shattered with horror when we see what can be done to Winston Smith.

Although effective as a satirical method, then, the beast allegory still does not allow Orwell to develop his characters beyond a one-dimensional level; for the most part, they signify one attribute or meaning. And it is not only the animals which exist in this way, but also the human characters. Farmer Jones, Frederick, and Pilkington, in fact, might be seen as burlesques of the Marxist conception of capitalism and fascism although one doubts if the irony extends this far. This one-dimensional aspect appears as a deficiency, as I have noted, in his novels. The white sahibs in *Burmese Days*, Reverend Hare of *A Clergyman's Daughter*, Ravelston in *Keep the Aspidistra Flying*, and Porteous of *Coming Up For Air*, among others are unconvincing because they are typecast rather than being presented with any complexity. The difference, of course, is that within *Animal Farm* this kind of characterization is at least functional, while in the realistic novel it reveals Orwell as incapable or unwilling to present the experience with any depth. Again, in the fable he found a form—limited in its demands and possibilities as it is—whose requirements he could satisfy.

But Orwell's success in establishing a formal unity notwithstanding, political realities cannot be accounted for in one-dimensional terms; and because the emotional experience is narrowed in *Animal Farm*, the ideas involved are of a less substantial nature. Certainly he dramatizes part of the truth of revolution, but not the whole of it. The dialectic between nature and civilization is rendered too simply here. He himself realized that no matter, much less a political idea, can be shaded black and white. Reality is neither that of the Yahoos nor the Houyhnhnms, but a third term which is a compound of the two. For Swift it was Gulliver. Ultimately, then, Orwell does achieve his intention in the satire; but the final value of any work cannot be predicated on its aesthetic coherence alone. If *Animal Farm* is an artistic success, it does not embody the significance of thought and feeling evident in some of his less finished books, for example his next novel, *Nineteen Eighty-Four*.

III

It is difficult to account for *Nineteen Eighty-Four's* imaginative and emotional power. It is a flawed novel: The plot, obvious, heavy-handed and melodramatic, reduces the major characters, Winston and Julia, to pawns; Martin O'Brien, the antagonist, emerges more like a parody of a science-fiction villain than a representative of an inhuman tyranny; and Orwell even resorts to the worn-out device, akin to the letter in the Victorian novel, of including a long essay on the history of Oceania and on politics, a serious structural defect. It exists, also, as an example of the author's distrust of the dramatic, evident in some way in almost all his works.

The major plot failure, a difficulty he had to a greater or lesser degree in all his novels, is that the principal action does not begin until Part II, a third of the way into the book. In Part I he deals with Winston's job in the Ministry of Truth, his first diary entries, and the description of Oceania. It is not until Part II that he and Julia begin their fated affair. The initial section parallels in manner and purpose the beginning of *Keep the Aspidistra Flying*, for example, in which Gordon Comstock is presented in detail. The result is the same in both novels: a certain tedium and wasted motion. In *Nineteen Eighty-Four*, furthermore, the explanatory nature and long build-up of Part I renders the plot itself fairly predictable. Thus the conflict between Winston and Julia and the Party, the inevitable force, is seriously weakened and the conclusion loses a necessary tragic dimension. It is, consequently, unmitigated pathos. In order to add interest to the plot, Orwell resorts to sensationalism, evident particularly in O'Brien's inquisition and Winston's torture.

Not only do the two main characters suffer because of the overabundance of machinery, but they themselves lack real depth and complexity. Orwell had, in a manner of speaking, painted himself into a corner. For the sake of the novel he required characters who possessed both the intelligence and will to revolt and yet, given the circumstances, they could be neither overly individualistic nor strong. Without question Winston is the more successful, for we can at least pity him. But it is impossible to feel anything for Julia. Unfortunately we tend to view her, like Winston does, as an object. The others, the Parsons, Mr. Charrington, the shopkeeper, the proles, and even O'Brien, remain faceless. A defense of his characterization on the basis that an individual personality would not be credible in this world is finally not to the point. More than in any other work of his fiction, Orwell simply sacrificed matters of plot and character to his obsession with idea. In *Nineteen Eighty-Four* it was not only a sense of urgency which led him to emphasize the polemic, but also the intriguing nature of the concept itself.

And yet it is precisely the idea and even his careful detailing of it, including the appendix, "The Principles of Newspeak," which explains to a great extent the novel's power. That art creates culture is nowhere more evident than in the case of *Nineteen Eighty-Four*. The date itself has definite relevance in Western civilization and not merely to those who have read the novel. It has became a general metaphor suggesting a certain kind of political state while calling up an emotion of apprehension about the future. The novel's social effect can be seen further in the common usage of such terms as "Big Brother," "Oceania," "doublethink," and "newspeak" to describe select contemporary conditions like government spending and its accompanying jargon. They connote what is waiting for us as a result of the continued growth of government. Orwell has created a language for us to think about both the present and the potentialities of the future. It is not only, then, his personal, moral sense and integrity which make him a conscience of our time, but also his art.

He of course did not so much create the idea of a universal slave state as define an inarticulate emotion that lay close to the surface of his culture. He did have antecedents, like Huxley's *Brave New World*— opposed in kind though it was to his own vision—and Eugene Zamiatin's *We*, the principal source of *Nineteen Eighty-Four*. But appearing, as the novel did, after the atomic bomb, during the first years of the

United Nations, and just as the Soviet Union was approaching full nuclear capability, it became an embodiment of all the postwar terrors. Its continuing popularity and relevance to the present political situation indicate that these same fears, although somewhat muted, are still very real in us.

A more important question in determining the novel's significance is whether its image of civilization's possibilities has anything more than a temporary value. Has Orwell touched a nerve unique to our own time? Or has he given expression to a universal anxiety about man's ability to control his own nature? It is an especially difficult question at this time, but ultimately, I believe, the novel is more than a historical oddity. In fact, it points to both a cultural phenomenon and one of man's fundamental preoccupations. If the utopian vision is indigenous to humanistic culture, so, paradoxically, is the tragic view. And if *Nineteen Eighty-Four* directly opposes the dream of human perfectibility, it also explicitly dramatizes the underlying but never realized dread of all tragedy. In the classic form of the tragedy, this dread: the doubt about man's essential worth, is put to rest—if not always easily—at least in the final movement; Orwell, on the other hand, carries the tragic uncertainty in his last novel to its logical and inevitable conclusion. And that end is shown most poignantly in the scene where O'Brien seeks to destroy Winston's belief in humanity. To confute him the inquisitor describes Winston's terrible emaciation, and then says, "'You are rotting away' . . ., 'you are falling to pieces. What are you? A bag of filth. Now turn round and look into that mirror. Do you see that thing facing you? That is the last man. If you are human, that is humanity. Now put your clothes on again'" (p. 278). In response Winston insists that he has at least maintained his integrity; he has not betrayed Julia. Because he is no longer convinced of his humanity, however, it is only a matter of time until he does.

Nineteen Eighty-Four, then, might be described as what Orwell calls a "good bad" book. In this category he places frankly escapist literature, but also novels which are serious in intent but lack artistic taste and coherence. More particularly, he cites *Uncle Tom's Cabin* "as the supreme example of the 'good bad' book. . . . It is an unintentionally ludicrous book, full of preposterous melodramatic incidents; it is also deeply moving and essentially true; it is hard to say which quality outweighs the other."[12] In other words, certain novels, and he puts those of Trollope, Dickens, and Dreiser in the group, succeed despite their aesthetic grossness because they possess "sheer skill, or native grace, which may have more survival value than erudition or intellectual power." He concludes, "I would back *Uncle Tom's Cabin* to outlive the complete works of Virginia Woolf or George Moore, though I know of no strictly literary test which would show where the superiority lies."

To be sure it is a poor literary test which places survival in the common culture as the supreme value. Orwell cannot define the quality which insures a work's continuance in the face of its own outrageous faults and is reduced to calling it "a sort of literary vitamin" or "native grace." He means, perhaps, what is identified by the equally unsatisfying phrase, "a sense of life or reality." *Nineteen Eighty-Four*, at any rate, does overcome its failure of plot and character, its imaginative vulgarity, and very well could survive as a "good bad" novel because it accurately presents an idea which corresponds to our universal and ever present fear of what we might become.

The annihilation of the spirit is, nevertheless, only one side of the novel's dialectic; on the other is that of the instinctual ego insisting on its own survival and selfish wants. And it is Orwell's development of this theme which remains as *Nineteen Eighty-Four's* artistic achievement. In the novel, as in all his work including the nonfiction, underlying the self's demand for freedom resides the idea that man, following his instincts, will find meaning.

But there is also the realization that for the individual to become completely himself, he must alleviate the horrible isolation of his rebellion through love, union with the non-self which is uncorrupted by society. John Flory mistakenly seeks it in Elizabeth; Dorothy Hare at least understands the need for others; Gordon Comstock accepts Rosemary and bourgeois values; the narrator of *Homage to Catalonia* and George Bowling attempt to find themselves in a closely knit community; Winston Smith sees in Julia another rebel and an opportunity to return to his natural self. Even in *The Road to Wigan Pier* Orwell celebrates the individual in the family where the nexus is human rather than cash. All fail, however, except Comstock and Bowling, who settle for a compromise. Flory, Dorothy, and Winston end in terrible isolation, the self dead or fragmented. Winston's final position is the worst, for he betrays his human loyalty and turns to Big Brother; he loves the machine.

Winston's and Julia's revolt is primarily sexual, a most appropriate metaphor of the individual's search for the primary self in a totally mechanical and non-personal environment. But their love-making, in the last analysis, has little to do with the higher, human emotions or even ordinary sensual pleasure: "In the old days, [Winston] thought, a man looked at a girl's body and saw that it was desirable, and that was the end of the story. But you could not have pure love or pure lust nowadays. No emotion was pure, because everything was mixed up with fear and hatred. Their embrace had been a battle, the climax a victory. It was a blow against the Party. It was a political act" (p. 130). Sexual intercourse for them is a drive to recover the biological self, the animal self, which radically opposes the Party's requirement of total impersonality. So their physical act recreates at least the tension between self and society. It is not really a human expression but simple copulation, which is nevertheless perfect rebellion, being nonrational, against pure mind. Winston rejoices therefore in Julia's animality:

> His heart leapt. Scores of times she had done it: he wished it had been hundreds—thousands. Anything that hinted at corruption always filled him with a wild hope. Who knew, perhaps the Party was rotten under the surface, its cult of strenuousness and self-denial simply a sham concealing iniquity. If he could have infected the whole lot of them with leprosy or syphilis, how

gladly he would have done so! Anything to rot, to weaken, to undermine! He pulled her down so that they were kneeling face to face.

"Listen. The more men you've had, the more I love you. Do you understand that?"

"Yes, perfectly."

"I hate purity, I hate goodness! I don't want any virtue to exist anywhere. I want everyone to be corrupt to the bones."

"Well then, I ought to suit you dear. I'm corrupt to the bones."

"You like doing this? I don't mean simply me: I mean the thing itself."

"I adore it."

That was above all what he wanted to hear. Not merely love of one person but the animal instinct, the simply undifferentiated desire: that was the force that would tear the Party to pieces. He pressed her down upon the grass, among the fallen bluebells. (pp. 129–130)

The primeval quality in their love-making links them with nature, the past, and the proles. Their meetings occur either in the country or in the secret room overlooking the proles' housing development and in full view of the washerwoman, a figure of gross fertility. For a time, then, they are able to create a separate world, symbolized by the paperweight Winston purchases from Mr. Charrington: "[The paperweight] was a heavy lump of glass, curved on one side, flat on the other, making almost a hemisphere. There was a peculiar softness, as of rainwater, in both the colour and the texture of the glass. At the heart of it, magnified by the curved surface, there was a strange, pink, convoluted object that recalled a rose or a sea anemone" (p. 99). Later Winston tells Julia that " 'It's a little chunk of history that they've forgotten to alter. It's a message from a hundred years ago, if one knew how to read it' " (p. 150). Then he looks deeply into it:

> The inexhaustibly interesting thing was not the fragment of coral but the interior of the glass itself. There was such a depth to it, and yet it was almost as transparent as air. It was as though the surface of the glass had been the arch of the sky, enclosing a tiny world with its atmosphere complete. He had the feeling that he could get inside it, and that in fact he was inside it, along with the mahogany bed and the gateleg table, and the clock and the steel engraving and the paperweight itself. The paperweight was the room he was in, and the coral was Julia's life and his own, fixed in a sort of eternity at the heart of the crystal. (p. 151)

Ironically, of course, their world is crystal, fragile, and transparent, but, still, for those moments, an individual one. Underneath, both Winston and Julia know that it is temporary but prefer the uncertainty rather than the Party or self-destruction: "In reality there was no escape. Even the one plan that was practicable, suicide, they had no intention of carrying out. To hang on from day to day and from week to week, spinning out the present that had no future, seemed an unconquerable instinct, just as one's lungs will always draw the next breath so long as there is air available" (p. 156).

The Party, however, realizes that the main threat to their power is not the intellect but the instincts;

therefore the Ministry of Love is responsible for law and order. It does not attempt to crush nature directly but to control it through isolation. Just as Winston and Julia are segregated from the society, so are the proles. The instincts alone are undisciplined energy, capable only of revolt, of anarchistic gestures, but not of revolution. Since they are only two and effectively kept apart from any community, they are doomed. The proles, on the other hand, form a real community which maintains the instincts inviolate. They remain impervious to the mind of the Party; bluntly, they are stupid but, as Winston sees, "By lack of understanding they remained sane. They simply swallowed everything, and what they swallowed did them no harm, because it left no residue behind, just as a grain of corn will pass undigested through the body of a bird" (p. 161). Their sanity, their insistence on self-preservation, ultimately manifests itself as communal morality. Just as the prole woman protests against the violent propaganda film in an effort to protect the children, so a man saves Winston from a bomb:

> "Steamer!" he yelled. "Look out, guv'nor! Bang over'-head! Lay down quick!"
>
> "Steamer" was a nickname which, for some reason, the proles applied to rocket bombs. Winston promptly flung himself on his face. The proles were nearly always right when they gave you a warning of this kind. They seemed to possess some kind of instinct which told them several seconds in advance when a rocket was coming, although the rockets supposedly travelled faster than sound. (p. 87)

If there is a hope, therefore, it must lie with the proles, since their individual instincts are directed by and protected in the community. But this time the drama of rebellion is resolved in favor of the machine. Winston and Julia are beaten before they begin; the real test would be between the proles and the Party. Even if it does not come, however, there is the assurance that the human spirit, if it will not achieve dominance, will endure.

If Orwell had maintained a dramatic concreteness, *Nineteen Eighty-Four* would undoubtedly have been a more coherent work of art. Yet there were matters, such as the history of Oceania, the rationale behind the slave state, and the political significance of the debasement of language, which he felt impelled to include for ideological reasons and which could only be treated through expository devices like Goldstein's book, O'Brien's long monologues and the essay on newspeak. He obviously thought that it was more important to describe how certain social phenomena present in postwar civilization resulted in Oceania rather than to work in concrete and personal terms. If he sacrificed aesthetic integrity and cogency by failing to completely unify the political and human centers of the novel, he managed to clearly articulate a complex idea of what was occurring in society, where it could lead, and, lastly, an effective antidote for the disease. Orwell, like D. H. Lawrence, was writing primarily for a middle-class audience and was intent on showing what they had lost in the pursuit of progress and how the loss of proletarian spontaneity, instinct, and community ends in the demolition of their precious individuality and of their civilization.

In many ways *Nineteen Eight-Four* stands as the culmination of his thought. Similarities of theme, atmosphere, character, and plot between it and preceding books indicate that Orwell's essential concept of reality varied little. The change took place not so much in his approach as in his growing confidence in what he saw and what he felt was required to effect a solution to cultural chaos. In fact, his last novel is his clearest, if not his most artistic, statement of his understanding of the central conflict in modern society. And if *Nineteen Eighty-Four* can be dismissed as art, it cannot be explained away as science fiction nor as the nightmare of a man in despair, for it seriously calls into question the very bases and assumptions of our entire way of thought and life.

IV

Of the many paradoxes confronting the critic of Orwell, the most complex is that while he did not produce either a significant body of art or a finished system of political thought, he remains one of the paramount figures in modern British literary history. Not only has he drawn as much or more critical attention than anyone of his generation, but he has had a substantial moral and intellectual influence on contemporary writers. Even in matters of form, many of today's artists are following his lead. To a great extent his pertinence may be accounted for by the fact that he is the most immediately relevant heir of the radical-

liberal tradition which has reacted against industrialism and mass civilization since the beginning of the
nineteenth century. Like his own idea of Dickens, he
was more a rebel than a revolutionary and essentially
a moralist rather than a political thinker. Although he
often called for a reordered social structure, he empha-
sized the necessity of maintaining traditional ethical
roots. The change he envisioned was not so much a
new system but an evolution of the present order.
Much like Matthew Arnold, for example, he sought
the best self of each class as the basis of a classless culture. He wanted to reestablish the traditional strengths
of English society, the morality of the yeoman, shopkeeper, and workingman and the intellectual acumen
of the middle class as a foundation of his socialism.

His intellectual ancestors, then, were nineteenth-
century radicals like William Cobbett, Dickens, and
William Morris and moderns like Thomas Hardy and
D. H. Lawrence, rather than Marx and Lenin. He is
also related to the enlightened, liberal thought of E.
M. Forster as well as Arnold. As diverse as these writers may have been in particulars, they shared a similar
attitude toward the development of industrial civilization; they recognized the substitution of the economic
for the personal nexus as disastrous and foresaw the
possibilities of cultural chaos unless some basis other
than the industrial could be found for the community.
In essence, however, they called for a transformation
of the self rather than of the system.[13]

To the young intellectuals of the thirties, after the
debacle of World War I, in the midst of the depression and during Hitler's rise, Cobbett's celebration of

rural England, Dickens's "change of heart," Arnold's and Morris's cultural dreams, Forster's philosophy of personal relations, and Lawrence's sexual ethic seemed hopelessly dated; better as material for the Cambridge Debating Union than as solutions for a social crisis of such magnitude. Orwell shared their belief that the nineteenth century's remedies for society were no longer adequate, but he did not turn in desperation, like many of them, to revolutionary communism. Indeed, as his thought developed he saw that no change could be brought about with any assurance of justice if one eliminates, as he states in "Fascism and Democracy," the healthy bases of liberal civilization. Such values as the objectivity of truth, the sanctity of the individual, and traditional moral standards could not be dispensed with, he insisted, unless one wanted another version of the Soviet Union or the Third Reich. Bourgeois democracy is not enough, but a just and equitable socialism, if it is to arrive, must be constructed on democracy's permanent values. Even though Orwell was faced with an obviously more dangerous political situation than that which confronted Arnold or Hardy or even Lawrence and though he realized that more drastic and immediate reformation was required than they proposed, he understood that their insistence on the radical centrality of the self must under no condition be disregarded. It was this native, bourgeois wisdom that protected him from the hysteria of commitment which nearly brought about, as he argues, Hitler's defeat of England.

During a period of transition when liberal democracy was obviously breaking up and society was moving toward another, as yet uncertain, form, Orwell attempted to shape a political idea with roots in the past that would also accommodate the needs of the present. There was no question in his mind that man in the mid-twentieth century was irrevocably a social being, that if he were to survive, in fact, he must commit himself to making a just society and combating the tyranny of any orthodoxy which would deprive him of his freedom. But the threat of a cataclysm never frightened him into the extremism of anarchistic individualism or the other extreme of a political philosophy which denied the self. It is his refusal to see the world in simplistic terms, his courage in attempting a synthesis of self and society, a synthesis, in short, of liberalism and Marxism which constitutes his contemporary relevance. I view Orwell's position in much the same way as Morton Zabel describes that of Lionel Trilling, who sees the necessity of bringing the liberal tradition to bear on modern politics:

> It *is* the will in modulation (Trilling contends) that must survive if absolutes are to be denied their tyranny and the intelligence is to survive for the use of justice and truth. The charge of defending "individual morality" against "social morality" is one that Mr. Trilling has not escaped in his experience of political controversy. This novel [*The Middle of the Journey*], with its subtle, athletic, and unsimplified articulation of "the double truth" of social and individual values shows how honestly he sees the complex actuality of values which the simplistic moralism of dogmatic or abstracting minds, hot for action and accusation, ignores.[14]

For the most part present-day British writers have recognized the validity of the same "double truth," shunning the romantic stance as well as ideological extremism; and since Orwell in his life and writing dramatized this so clearly, he persists for them as a forceful moral and artistic guide.[15] Like Gordon Comstock, the "semi-heroes" of Kingsley Amis, John Wain, Alan Sillitoe, Raymond Williams, and John Braine, for example, see only emotional death in isolation and strain to make a connection, no matter how tentative, with society. Inherent in much of their fiction is Orwell's idea that personal values are not sufficient, indeed are not possible unless one eliminates the span between the self and culture. None of their characters are absolutely successful, but even when they fail, they see that it is necessary to create the relationship. Even though the society is a destructive jungle, protagonists like Arthur Seaton in *Saturday Night and Sunday Morning*, Charles Lumley in *Hurry on Down*, and Peter Owen in *Second Generation* apprehend the fact that for the sake of their own moral and spiritual health they must accept sociality.

Since one of the chief insights to emerge from contemporary experience is that the person is unalterably a social being and the principal problem is how to make contact with an essentially hostile environment and yet retain one's individuality, for most writers the realistic novel appears as the appropriate form. Here again they are at one with Orwell, with the important difference that today's novelists are, on the whole, more successful, even though they are faced with the same problem of dramatizing social ideas. The answer is not simply that they are better craftsmen, although this is a major part of it. But this brings us to a final evaluation of Orwell's search for an artistic form.

His attempt to find or create a form in which he could combine his polemic and artistic intentions did not really succeed, as I have shown, except in the case of *Animal Farm*. Just as he gave no final coherence to his political thought, neither did he resolve his problems as an artist. Orwell's failure occurred because he did not allow his ideas to develop from the characters and action but tended to impose and interject them. In his discussion of *Nineteen Eighty-Four*, George Woodcock defines the book's weakness as the author's inability to unite the human and theoretical centers.[16] The deficiency of all his works, fiction as well as nonfiction, can be traced to the same source, for he essentially mistrusted the dramatic imagination to carry his message.

The reason behind his lack of confidence also accounts for his inability to establish an ultimately satisfying political and artistic idea: The fact that he lived in a transitional period of great danger brought about political pressures that he was not equipped as a man or as an artist to handle. Like many of his generation he had neither the political experience nor the education to deal with violent social upheavals and the threat of brutal and oppressive dictatorships. In his poem "A Happy Vicar," written in 1935, he describes his longing for the eighteenth century and his sense of displacement: that neither he nor anyone was born for an age of industrialism and commissars.[17] In *Homage to Catalonia*, speaking of the Spaniards he met during the Civil War, he says, "They have . . . a generosity, a species of nobility, that do not really belong to the twentieth century" (p. 239). Indeed, the drama of the book suggests that ironically this nobility left the Spaniards vulnerable to the agents of the commissars in Barcelona. No matter how hard he tried to become "George Orwell," the contemporary man struggling with his age, he always retained something of Eric Blair, a man out of his time and place. The present often overwhelmed him, most dramatically in Spain but also immediately before the war when he was writing *Coming Up For Air* and afterwards when he was working on *Nineteen Eighty-Four*.

At times like this his reaction, prompted by a sense of urgency, was often to sacrifice the integrity of his work for the sake of the discursive message. Analogously, he felt there was no leisure to order his political thought; the first task, he insisted, was to combat the Soviet and German tyrannies and to eliminate poverty. To be sure, novelists at the moment live in a potentially more perilous age than his, but also there is time, or at least there seems to be, to think about the problems of art and politics which an era demanding commitment creates. Moreover, the experience of the thirties and forties, communicated by writers like Orwell, have made the world of commissars and atomic weapons a less alien one. In a very real way, he taught the next generation about a world that no one was born for but that everyone must learn to live in.

He not only revealed our world in his art, however; he also demonstrated a way to avoid the devastating fate he imagined for us: If we refuse to accept the illusion of the whale, the illusion of security in any state or ideology, and are willing to risk our last wager on the self, the root and foundation of our civilization, then we can do more than survive. This process of wrenching the self free from the deceptive safety of any hole-and-corner, the agonizing rebirth that he himself underwent and symbolically indicated by changing his name, was for him the prelude and basis for wholeness, for relationship, for community which would provide the strength to prevail. Unfortunately when his commitment to found a community or his terror of the present interfered with his art, the results were a simplification of reality and outright propaganda. Yet for all the dissatisfaction one feels with him as an artist, one cannot ignore that he managed, because of his involvement, to add a human dimension to a historical era which would otherwise have remained an abstraction, a mass of political issues, rather than the intense personal struggle it was. So it is not only George Orwell's life, that drama made valuable by his refusal to despair in man, but also his art which guarantees his permanency in our civilization.

Notes

Whenever possible and for the sake of convenience I have used *The Collected Essays, Journalism and Letters of George Orwell* (Volume I, *An Age Like This: 1920–1940*; Volume II, *My Country Right or Left: 1940–1943*; Volume III, *As I Please: 1943–1945*; Volume IV, *In Front of Your Nose: 1945–1950*), edited by Sonia Orwell and Ian Angus (New York: Harcourt, Brace & World, 1968) rather than the original sources. For Orwell's novels and the longer non-fiction I have employed the uniform edition published by Secker & Warburg, London, and cited the original publication dates in the text and the Bibliography.

NOTES TO INTRODUCTION

1. (New York: Viking, Compass Book Edition, 1964), p. 159.

2. *Mr. Sammler's Planet* (New York: Viking, 1970), p. 46.

NOTES TO CHAPTER ONE

1. "W. B. Yeats," *My Country Right or Left*, pp. 273–274.

2. "Inside the Whale," *An Age Like This*, p. 515. Also note what C. Day Lewis says in his autobiography: "We had all, I think, lapsed from the Christian faith, and tended to despair of Liberalism as an effective instrument

for dealing with the problems of our day, if not to despise
it as an outworn creed. Innoculated against Roman Ca-
tholicism by the religion of my youth, I simply felt the
need for a faith which had the authority, the logic, the
cut-and-driedness of the Roman Church—a faith which
would fill the void left by the leaking away of traditional
religion, would make sense of our troubled times and make
real demands on me. Marxism appeared to fill the bill. It
appealed too, I imagine, to the part of me which, from
time to time revolted against the intolerable burden of self-
hood and desired the anonymity of a unit in a crowd. My
Communism, then, had a religious quality." *The Buried
Day* (New York: Harper & Brothers, 1960), p. 209.

3. "Why I Write," *An Age Like This*, p. 5.

4. Ibid., p. 269.

5. Greene, *Journey Without Maps* (London: Heineman
Uniform Edition, 1947), p. 310. All subsequent references
are to this edition with the pagination indicated in
the text.

6. *In Front of Your Nose*, p. 63.

7. *As I Please*, p. 103.

8. It appears, however, that Orwell was rather an extraordinary schoolboy. According to Cyril Connolly, at
Eton Orwell was extremely individualistic and sensitive.
During World War I he astounded his classmates by forecasting that England would be a much weaker nation after
the conflict, which, of course, turned out to be highly accurate. Connolly relates another story, demonstrating Orwell's early maturity. He says, "I remember a moment
under a fig-tree in one of the boulevards of the seaside
town, Orwell striding beside me and saying in his flat,
ageless voice: 'You know, Connolly, there's only one
remedy for all diseases.' I felt the usual guilty tremor when
sex was mentioned and hazarded, 'You mean going to the

lavatory?' 'No—I mean Death.' " *Enemies of Promise* (New York: Macmillan, 1948), p. 164.

9. "Such, Such Were the Joys," *In Front of Your Nose*, p. 360. All subsequent references are to this text with the pagination indicated in the text.

10. *My Country Right or Left*, p. 164.

11. *An Age Like This*, p. 242.

12. *The Road to Wigan Pier* (London: Secker & Warburg, 1959), pp. 149–150. All subsequent references are to this edition with the pagination indicated in the text.

13. *A Clergyman's Daughter* (London: Secker & Warburg, 1960), p. 316. All subsequent references are to this edition with the pagination indicated in the text.

14. Rees, *George Orwell: Fugitive from the Camp of Victory* (London: Secker & Warburg, 1961), p. 138.

15. Hollis, *A Study of George Orwell: The Man and His Works* (Chicago: Regnery, 1956), p. 74.

16. Rees, p. 135.

17. Fyvel, "George Orwell and Eric Blair: Glimpses of a Dual Life," *Encounter* XIII (July 1959), 60–65. Orwell's conversion to the working class was not accomplished without a modicum of snobbery and self-righteousness—perhaps a common denominator of all conversions. John Morris tells a story in which he and Orwell went into a pub together. Orwell asked Morris what he wanted and he answered, "Beer." The former looked at him strangely and when the waitress arrived ordered a pint of bitters for himself and the beer for Morris. Disturbed by Orwell's attitude, Morris asked him, once they left, about his reaction. He replied that one doesn't ask for a beer in a working man's bar; it reveals, he said, one's middle-class origins. Morris asserted, however, that he was in fact middle-class —like Orwell himself. Orwell ended the exchange by telling his companion that it was bad manners to let it be

known in this situation. " 'Some Are More Equal Than Others': A Note on George Orwell," in *Penguin New Writing*, ed. John Lehmann, XL (Harmondsworth, England, 1950), 90–97.

18. Trilling, "George Orwell and the Politics of Truth," *The Opposing Self: Nine Essays in Criticism* (New York: Viking, 1955), p. 162.

19. *The Road to Wigan Pier* (London: Victor Gollancz Ltd., 1937), pp. xi–xxiv.

20. Rees, p. 136.

21. *Homage to Catalonia* (London: Secker & Warburg, 1959), p. 4. All subsequent references are to this edition with the pagination indicated in the text.

22. Rieff, "George Orwell and the Post-Liberal Imagination," *Kenyon Review* XVI (Winter 1954), 49–70.

23. *As I Please*, p. 64.

24. Brander, *George Orwell* (London: Longmans, 1954), p. 32.

25. *An Age Like This*, p. 309.

26. Orwell excluded the essay when he collected *Critical Essays* (1946), which indicates to Brander, *op. cit.*, p. 45, that he no longer at that point shared its pessimism.

27. *My Country Right or Left*, pp. 339–450.

28. *Coming Up For Air* (London: Secker & Warburg, 1948), pp. 109–110. All subsequent references are to this edition with the pagination indicated in the text.

29. Thale, "Orwell's Modest Proposal," *Critical Quarterly* IX (1962), 365–368.

30. *The Lion and the Unicorn: Socialism and the English Genius* (London: Secker & Warburg, 1962), p. 39. All subsequent references are to this edition with pagination indicated in the text.

31. *My Country Right or Left*, p. 141.

32. Forster, *Two Cheers for Democracy* (New York: Harcourt, Brace & World, 1951), p. 75.

33. *The Betrayal of the Left*, ed. Victor Gollancz (London: Gollancz, 1941), pp. 214–215.

34. "London Letter," *As I Please*, p. 294.

35. *My Country Right or Left*, pp. 352, 367.

36. Symons, "Orwell, A Reminiscence," *London Magazine* III (September 1963), 33–49.

37. *In Front of Your Nose*, p. 443.

38. *My Country Right or Left*, p. 266.

39. *In Front of Your Nose*, pp. 216–217.

40. *Animal Farm* (London: Secker & Warburg, 1945), p. 87. All subsequent references are to this edition with pagination indicated in the text.

41. "Arthur Koestler," *As I Please*, p. 244.

42. *As I Please*, p. 384.

43. Ibid., p. 88.

44. Ibid., p. 266.

45. Orwell, "The British General Election," *Commentary* I (November 1945), 65–70.

46. *Nineteen Eighty-Four* (London: Secker & Warburg, 1949), p. 227. All subsequent references are to this edition with pagination indicated in the text.

47. Brander, p. 196.

48. Howe, "Orwell: History as Nightmare," *Politics and the Novel* (New York: Horizon Press, 1956), p. 237.

49. In a letter to Francis A. Henson of the United Automobile Workers, Orwell answered questions prompted by *Nineteen Eighty-Four*. He said: "My recent novel is NOT intended as an attack on Socialism or on the British Labour Party (of which I am a supporter) but as a show-up of the perversions to which a centralised economy is liable and which have already been partly realised in Communism and Fascism. I do not believe that the kind of society I

describe necessarily *will* arrive, but I believe (allowing of course for the fact that the book is a satire) that something resembling it *could* arrive. I believe also that totalitarian ideas have taken root in the minds of intellectuals everywhere, and I have tried to draw these ideas out to their logical consequences. The scene of the book is laid in Britain in order to emphasise that the English-speaking races are not innately better than anyone else and that totalitarianism, *if not fought against*, could triumph anywhere." *In Front of Your Nose*, p. 502.

50.   John O. Lyons, "George Orwell's Opaque Glass in *1984*," *Wisconsin Studies in Contemporary Literature* II (Fall 1961), 39–46.

51.   *In Front of Your Nose*, p. 372.

52.   Rees, p. 142.

53.   Tom Hopkinson, "George Orwell—Darkside Out," *Cornhill* CLXVI (Summer 1953), 450–470.

54.   See George Woodcock, *The Crystal Spirit: A Study of George Orwell* (Boston and Toronto: Little, Brown, 1966), p. 43. Woodcock contends that Orwell went to Jura seeking renewal rather than death.

55.   Rieff, pp. 49–70.

56.   Orwell, "Britain's Struggle for Survival," *Commentary* VI (October 1948), 343–349.

NOTES TO CHAPTER TWO

1.   These ideas form the basic assumption of Trilling's *The Liberal Imagination* (New York: Viking, 1950) and are made explicit in the essays, "Reality in America," "Manners, Morals and the Novel," "Art and Fortune," and "The Meaning of a Literary Idea," which are contained in that volume. He sees the "dominant, critical attitude" of

our time as developing from T. S. Eliot's theories of literature, especially his concept of the "objective correlative." In the United States, the "new criticism" in its first stages is, of course, connected with John Crowe Ransom, Allen Tate, Cleanth Brooks and other so-called "agrarians." In such studies as *Matthew Arnold, E. M. Forster, The Opposing Self,* and *Beyond Culture,* Trilling has shown himself to be the most articulate modern critic in explaining the relationship between literature and ideas.

2. "The Frontiers of Art and Propaganda," *My Country Right or Left,*" p. 126.

3. *An Age Like This,* p. 448.

4. Ibid., p. 6.

5. Ibid.

6. Ibid.

7. Ibid., p. 7.

8. Frederick R. Karl, "George Orwell: The White Man's Burden," *A Reader's Guide to the Contemporary English Novel* (New York: Noonday, 1962), pp. 148–166.

9. *The Road to Wigan Pier,* p. 153.

10. *Down and Out in Paris and London* (London: Secker & Warburg, 1949), p. 213. All subsequent references are to this edition with pagination indicated in the text.

11. *In Front of Your Nose,* p. 422.

12. Avril Dunn, "My Brother, George Orwell," *Twentieth Century* CLXIX (March 1961), 255–261.

13. John Wain, "George Orwell," *Essays on Literature and Ideas* (London: Macmillan, 1963), p. 180.

14. *Burmese Days* (London: Secker & Warburg, 1961), p. 5. All subsequent references are to this edition with pagination indicated in the text.

15. See "Hop-Picking," *An Age Like This,* pp. 52–71, a diary Orwell kept in which he recorded his experiences

among the Cockney hop-pickers in Kent during August and September of 1931.

16. *My Country Right or Left*, p. 240.

17. "Charles Dickens," *An Age Like This*, p. 460.

NOTES TO CHAPTER THREE

1. FitzGibbon, *The Life of Dylan Thomas* (Boston and Toronto: Little, Brown, 1965), p. 151. See also Rayner Heppenstall, *Four Absentees* (London: Barrie & Rockcliff, 1960) for an account—although a somewhat bitter one—of Orwell's Soho days.

2. *Keep the Aspidistra Flying*, (London: Secker & Warburg, 1954), p. 258. All subsequent references are to this edition with the pagination indicated in the text.

3. Wain, " 'Here Lies Lower Binfield': On George Orwell," *Encounter* XVII (October 1961), 70–83.

4. Edrich, "Naïveté and Simplicity in Orwell's Writing: *Homage to Catalonia*," *University of Kansas City Review* XXVII (June 1961), 289–297.

5. Mander, "One Step Forward: Two Steps Back," *The Writer and Commitment* (London: Secker & Warburg, 1961), p. 81.

NOTES TO CHAPTER FOUR

1. Orwell's benefactor was L. H. Myers, the novelist. Richard Rees, *George Orwell: Fugitive from the Camp of Victory*, p. 69.

2. Woodcock, *The Crystal Spirit*, p. 187.

3. *My Country Right or Left*, p. 163.

4. *In Front of Your Nose*, p. 422.

5. *An Age Like This*, pp. 377–378.

6. See Edward M. Thomas, *Orwell* (Edinburgh and London: Oliver & Boyd, 1965), p. 28, for a somewhat different phrasing of this idea.

7. *An Age Like This*, p. 392.

8. Trilling, "Freud: Within and Beyond Culture," *Beyond Culture: Essays on Literature and Learning* (New York: Viking, 1965), p. 115.

9. Woodcock, pp. 63–64.

10. *An Age Like This*, pp. 518–519.

11. C. M. Woodhouse, Introduction to *Animal Farm* (New York: Signet Classic Edition, n.d.), p. xxi.

12. "Good Bad Books," *In Front of Your Nose*, pp. 21–22.

13. See Raymond Williams, *Culture and Society: 1780–1950* (New York: Columbia University Press, 1958) for a full interpretation of the tradition and Orwell's relationship to it. Also see T. A. Birrel, "Is Integrity Enough?: A Study of George Orwell," *Dublin Review* CCXXIV, No. 449 (Fall 1950), pp. 49–65.

14. Zabel, "The Straight Way Lost," *Craft and Character in Modern Fiction* (New York: Viking, 1957), p. 317.

15. Robert Conquest, the poet and critic, has said: "If one had briefly to distinguish the poetry of the fifties from its predecessors, I believe the most important general point would be that it submits to no great systems of theoretical constructs nor agglomerations of unconscious commands. It is free from both mystical and logical compulsions and —like modern philosophy—is empirical in its attitude to all that comes. This reverence for the real person or event is, indeed, a part of the general intellectual ambience (in so far as that is not blind or retrogressive) of our time. One might, without stretching matters too far, say that George

Orwell with his principle of real, rather than ideological, honesty, exerted, even though indirectly, one of the major influences on modern poetry. "Introduction," *New Lines, An Anthology* (London: Macmillan, 1956), pp. xiv–xv.

16. Woodcock, p. 349.

17. "A Happy Vicar" is reprinted in "Why I Write," *An Age Like This*, pp. 4–5.

Bibliography

The publishers and dates given in Part I refer to the original editions of Orwell's works. I have limited my selection of critical works on Orwell (Part II) to full-length treatments, those mentioned in the text, and those I find of particular interest. Readers seeking a fuller bibliography should consult Zeke and White, *George Orwell: A Selected Bibliography* and the annual bibliography of the Modern Language Association.

Part I

Down and Out in Paris and London. London: Gollancz, 1933.

Burmese Days. New York: Harper, 1934. (London: Gollancz, 1935).

A Clergyman's Daughter. London: Gollancz, 1935.

Keep the Aspidistra Flying. London: Gollancz, 1936.

The Road to Wigan Pier. London: Gollancz, 1937.

Homage to Catalonia. London: Secker & Warburg, 1938.

Coming Up For Air. London: Gollancz, 1939.

The Lion and the Unicorn: Socialism and the English Genus. London: Secker & Warburg, 1941.

Animal Farm. London: Secker & Warburg, 1945.

James Burnham and the Managerial Revolution. London: Socialist Books, 1946.

Critical Essays. London: Secker & Warburg, 1946 (published in New York as *Dickens, Dali and Others*, Harcourt, Brace & World, 1946).

The English People. London: Collins, 1947.

Nineteen Eighty-Four. London: Secker & Warburg, 1949.

Shooting an Elephant and Other Essays. London: Secker & Warburg, 1950.

England Your England. London: Secker & Warburg, 1953.

Such, Such Were the Joys. New York: Harcourt, Brace & World, 1953. (Similar to *England Your England* but includes the long autobiographical title essay).

Collected Essays. London: Secker & Warburg, 1961.

The Collected Essays, Journalism and Letters of George Orwell (Volume I, *An Age Like This: 1920–1940*; Volume II, *My Country Right Or Left 1940–1943*; Volume III, *As I Please: 1943–1945*; Volume IV, *In Front of Your Nose: 1945–1950*). Edited by Sonia Orwell and Ian Angus. New York: Harcourt, Brace & World, 1968.

Part II

ALLDRITT, KEITH. *The Making of George Orwell: An Essay in Literary History*. New York: St. Martin's Press, 1969.

ATKINS, JOHN. *George Orwell: A Literary Study*. London: Calder, 1954.

BIRREL, T. A. "Is Integrity Enough?" *Dublin Review* CCXXIV, No. 449 (Fall 1950), 49–55.

BRANDER, LAURENCE. *George Orwell*. London: Longmans, 1954.

CALDER, JENNI. *Chronicles of Conscience: A Study of George Orwell and Arthur Koestler*. Pittsburgh: University of Pittsburgh Press, 1968.

CONNOLLY, CYRIL. *Enemies of Promise*. New York: Macmillan, 1948.

CONQUEST, ROBERT, ed. *New Lines, An Anthology*. London: Macmillan, 1956.

DAY LEWIS, C. *The Buried Day*. New York: Harper & Brothers, 1960.

DUNN, AVRIL. "My Brother, George Orwell." *Twentieth Century* CLXIX (March 1961), 255–261.

EDRICH, EMANUEL. "Naïveté and Simplicity in Orwell's Writing: *Homage to Catalonia*." *University of Kansas City Review* XXVII (Summer 1961), 289–297.

FEN, ELISAVITA. "George Orwell's First Wife." *Twentieth Century* CLXVIII (August 1960), 115–126.

FITZGIBBON, CONSTANTINE. *The Life of Dylan Thomas*. Boston and Toronto: Little, Brown, 1965.

FORSTER, E. M. "George Orwell." In *Two Cheers for Democracy*, by E. M. Forster, pp. 60–63. New York: Harcourt, Brace & World, 1951.

FYVEL, T. R. "George Orwell and Eric Blair: Glimpses of a Dual Life." *Encounter* XIII (July 1959), 60–65.

GOLLANCZ, VICTOR. Foreword to *The Road to Wigan Pier*. London: Gollancz, 1937.

GREENBLATT, STEPHEN JAY. *Three Modern Satirists: Waugh, Orwell, and Huxley*. New Haven: Yale University Press, 1965.

GREENE, GRAHAM. *Journey Without Maps*. London: Heineman, 1947.

GROSS, MIRIAM, ed. *The World of George Orwell*. New York: Simon & Shuster, 1972.

HEPPENSTALL, RAYNER. *Four Absentees*. London: Barrie & Rockcliff, 1960.

HOLLIS, CHRISTOPHER. *A Study of George Orwell: The Man and His Works*. Chicago: Henry Regnery, 1956.

HOPKINSON, TOM. "George Orwell—Darkside Out." *Cornhill* CLXVI (Summer, 1953), 450–470.

HOWE, IRVING. "Orwell: History as Nightmare." In *Politics and the Novel*, by Irving Howe, pp. 235–251. New York: Horizon, 1956.

KARL, FREDERICK. "George Orwell: The White Man's Burden." *A Reader's Guide to the Contemporary English Novel,* by Frederick Karl, pp. 148–166. New York: The Noonday Press, 1962.

LEE, ROBERT A. *Orwell's Fiction.* Notre Dame and London: University of Notre Dame Press, 1969.

LIEF, RUTH ANN. *Homage to Catalonia: The Prophetic Vision of George Orwell.* Columbus: Ohio State University Press, 1969.

LYONS, JOHN O. "George Orwell's Opaque Glass in *1984.*" *Wisconsin Studies in Contemporary Literature* II (Fall 1961), 39–46.

MANDER, JOHN. "One Step Forward: Two Steps Back." In *The Writer and Commitment,* by John Mander, pp. 71–110. London: Secker & Warburg, 1961.

MORRIS, JOHN. " 'Some Are More Equal than Others': A Note on George Orwell." In *Penguin New Writing,* edited by John Lehmann, LX, pp. 90–97. Harmondsworth, England, 1960.

OXLEY, B. T. *George Orwell.* London: Evans Brothers, 1967.

REES, RICHARD. *George Orwell: Fugitive from the Camp of Victory.* London: Secker & Warburg, 1961.

RIEFF, PHILIP. "George Orwell and the Post-Liberal Imagination." *Kenyon Review* XVI (Winter 1954), 49–70.

SYMONS, JULIAN. "Orwell, A Reminiscence." *London Magazine* III (September 1963), 33–49.

THALE, JEROME. "Orwell's Modest Proposal." *Critical Quarterly* IX (1962), 365–368.

THOMAS, EDWARD M. *Orwell.* Edinburgh and London: Oliver & Boyd, 1965.

TRILLING, LIONEL. "George Orwell and the Politics of Truth." In *The Opposing Self: Nine Essays in Criticism,* by Lionel Trilling, pp. 151–172. New York: Viking, 1955.

VOORHEES, RICHARD J. *The Paradox of George Orwell.* West Lafayette, Indiana: Purdue University Studies, 1961.

WAIN, JOHN. " 'Here Lies Lower Binfield': On George Orwell," *Encounter* XVII (October 1961), 70–83.

————. "George Orwell." In *Essays on Literature and Ideas,* by John Wain, pp. 180–213. London: Macmillan, 1963.

WILLIAMS, RAYMOND. "George Orwell." In *Culture and Society, 1780–1950,* by Raymond Williams, pp. 258–294. New York: Columbia University Press, 1958.

————. *George Orwell.* New York: Viking, 1971.

WOODCOCK, GEORGE. *The Crystal Spirit: A Study of George Orwell.* Boston and Toronto: Little, Brown, 1966.

WOODHOUSE, C. M. Introduction to *Animal Farm.* New York: Signet edition, n.d.

YORKS, SAMUEL A. "George Orwell: Seer Over His Shoulder." *Bucknell Review* IX (March 1960), 23–45.

ZABEL, MORTON. "The Straight Way Lost." In *Craft and Character in Modern Fiction,* by Morton Zabel. New York: Viking, 1957.

ZEKE, ZOLTAN G. and WHITE, WILLIAM. *George Orwell: A Selected Bibliography.* Boston: Boston Linotype Print, 1962.

Index